D1606154

Kittens

Complete Care
Made Easy
TM

Kittens

A Guide to Caring for Your Kitten

By Sandy Meyer
Photographs by Isabelle Francais

BOWTIE
P R E S S ®

Irvine, California

Karla Austin, *Business Operations Manager*
Nick Clemente, *Special Consultant*
Barbara Kimmel, *Editor*
Jackie Franza, *Consulting Editor*
Honey Winters, *Designer*
Indexed by Melody Englund

The kittens in this book are referred to as *he* and *she* in alternating chapters unless their gender is apparent from the activity discussed.

Photographs Copyright © 2006 by Isabelle Francais. Photographs on pages 17, 41, 62, 73, 81, 121, 136, and 139 Copyright © 2006 by Maureen Blaney Flietner.

Text Copyright © 2006 by BowTie Press®

All rights reserved. No part of this book may be reproduced, stored in a retrieval system, or transmitted in any form or by any means, electronic, mechanical, photocopying, recording, or otherwise, without the prior written permission of BowTie Press®, except for the inclusion of brief quotations in an acknowledged review.

Library of Congress Cataloging-in-Publication Data

Meyer, Sandy.
  Kittens : a guide to caring for your kitten / Sandy Meyer ; photographs by Isabelle Francais.
     p. cm.— (Complete care made easy)
  Includes index.
  ISBN 1-931993-77-7
  1. Kittens. I. Title. II. Series.

  SF447.M488 2006
  636.8'07—dc22
              2006002160

BowTie Press®
A Division of BowTie, Inc.
3 Burroughs
Irvine, California 92618

Printed and bound in Singapore
Second printing in 2007:
10 09 08 07   2 3 4 5 6 7 8 9 10

Acknowledgments

IN WRITING THIS BOOK, I DISCOVERED HOW MUCH I HAVE learned over the years from the excellent writers and editors at *Cat Fancy* magazine. I'm grateful to Susan Logan, my friend and supervisor, for recommending me for this incredible project. My heartfelt thanks go to dear friends and family for their support and encouragement and to my patient editors for their guidance. Of course, special thanks go to the wonderful cats and kittens who have shared my home and life—especially Tripper, who spent many nights beside me during this project.

—Sandy Meyer

Contents

CHAPTER

1

Understanding Kittens

Contrary to popular belief, cats are not cool and aloof loners. If you give your kitten plenty of love and affection, she will return it to you in kind.

Y OU ARE IN GOOD COMPANY WHEN IT COMES TO bringing a kitten into your household. Kitten ownership is on the rise, as evidenced in the 2005–2006 American Pet Product Manufacturers Association (APPMA) National Pet Owners Survey. And why not? Soft, curious, and overflowing with energy, a kitten's adorable antics are bound to warm your heart and keep a smile on your face.

Kittens make great additions to households when owners make an effort to match the kittens' personalities to their own lifestyles. And, with proper care, you will have a friend for years because cats often live into their twenties. So read on to arm yourself with information and get excited about your upcoming kitten adventures!

The Truth About Cats

The relationship between cats and humans has ebbed and flowed for thousands of years. They were once partners, then enemies, and finally friends. During the ups and downs, myths and folklore have become intertwined with truth, causing some serious misconceptions about cats. To get off on the right foot, let's clear up some of the confusion right now.

Independent and mysterious, cats like this Russian blue kitten have been part of our myths and fanciful tales for centuries.

Myth 1: Cats have nine lives.

As a species, cats are very prolific and resilient. They are survivors. However, each individual cat is small and vulnerable in a world full of dangers. As with all other creatures, human and otherwise, cats have only one life to live. They, too, are susceptible to disease, injury, and death. Although proper care and consideration can add years and quality to a cat's life, she does not receive nine opportunities to get it right.

Myth 2: Cats are like dogs.

Cats and dogs are different species. It's true that dogs and cats share some similarities: both mammals have four legs, and most have hair over their bodies and possess tails. Many cats play fetch, just as many dogs do. However, these two animals have extremely different instincts. One of the most obvious differences is their social structure. Dogs are pack animals. They need to be part of a pack, and they depend on that group. Cats, on the other hand, are solitary hunters, taking care of themselves. Although cats can and do learn to live together peaceably, cats require adequate territories of their own. They need personal space and for that space to be respected.

Myth 3: Cats are an inexpensive and low-maintenance alternative to dogs.

The only inexpensive and low-maintenance cat is a neglected one. Both cats and dogs need a quality diet, regular veterinary visits, and daily care and attention. Although your cat doesn't need to be walked for exercise or to relieve herself, she does need mental and physical stimulation to keep her healthy. The only way your cat may be less expensive than a dog is if you are comparing the cat to a large dog breed. The larger the animal, the more food she eats and the larger medication dosage she would receive.

Myth 4: Cats are unfriendly and solitary animals.

Many people mistake the cat's independence for unfriendliness. Some cats are fussier about whom they choose to spend their time with, but most are communicative and affectionate with their chosen people. Once cats understand that their basic survival needs—shelter, food, and water—will be consistently met, they can move on to luxuries such as human companionship. Many house cats meet their owners at the door when arriving home from school or work, follow their owners around the home, and sleep in their owners' rooms and on their beds, if allowed. However, most cats are also quite comfortable spending time alone sunning in favorite spots and taking catnaps in quiet, solitary corners. There is a wonderful balance between socializing and meditating in the life of a cat.

Myth 5: Cats must have access to the outdoors to be truly happy.

Although it can be challenging to teach an outdoor cat that the indoors really is the best place to be, most cats adjust quite well. Cats are hunters by nature, but they do not require live prey to satisfy their hunting needs. Indoor-only cats live happy, satisfying lives with the help of their owners. And this indoor-only lifestyle reduces and eliminates countless dangers from such things as automobiles, cruel human behaviors, deadly chemicals, and threats from other animals. With a little patience, creativity, and

These two kittens are content to be indoors, where they have food, shelter, and plenty of opportunities for play and interaction.

consistency, you can transform your cat's life into a full, indoor-only lifestyle. And you will be providing your precious pet with a longer, healthier life.

Myth 6: Cats always land (unharmed) on their feet.

Cats do possess an amazing self-righting reflex. The falling cat's brain quickly figures out her position in space; then she turns her head and front limbs toward the ground. Her flexible spine aligns with the rest of her body, and her limbs spread out like a parachute to prepare for the landing. From short heights, flexible joints and floating collarbones soften the shock of the cat's arrival on the ground. But a fall from six stories or higher is almost always fatal. And even a short fall can mean the self-righting reflex does not have time to fully protect the cat from injuries or worse.

Myth 7: Cats become fat and lazy when spayed or neutered.

It's true that cats' metabolisms can slow after they have been fixed, but these important surgeries do not cause cats to become fat and lazy. With the veterinarian's help, owners can adjust their cats' food intake to accommodate the slower metabolisms. Owners can also create more physical stimulation in their cats' daily lives. Moving the food bowl upstairs or onto a counter so the cat must exert energy to get there is a simple way to keep a cat active. Daily play sessions that encourage the cat to get up and moving will also help.

Myth 8: Female cats need to have one litter before getting spayed.

Aside from contributing to the cat overpopulation problem and causing your pet unnecessary discomfort, putting off spaying your cat until after her first litter increases her chances of developing health problems including uterine, ovarian, and breast cancers. There is no reason to put this surgery off, and you already have three important reasons for getting it done immediately.

Myth 9: Cats and babies do not mix.

Fears about cats giving unborn babies diseases and stealing the breath of infants abound, even in today's modern society. Toxoplasmosis, an infection caused by a parasite called *toxoplasma*

Breeding should be a deliberate choice and made with the knowledge that there are homes for all the kittens produced. If you do not intend to breed, get your kitten spayed early.

gondii, can harm an unborn baby under certain conditions. Cats are often blamed for this disease, and some people in the medical community still urge pregnant women to get rid of their cats. However, most cases of toxoplasmosis occur when pregnant women have eaten undercooked meats; dairy products that have not been pasteurized; or raw, unwashed vegetables. There is a small risk to cat owners who are pregnant, but it's very easy to reduce the risk without getting rid of the cat: have a nonpregnant friend or family member take over litter box duties, always wear gloves when gardening (feral, stray, and other outdoor cats may have used your garden as a bathroom), and scrub and peel all root vegetables.

And cats cannot steal a baby's breath, nor do they try to. Cats may be curious about the new little person and the baby's new smells and sounds. Also, the baby's milky breath and remnants of the latest meal around the lips may attract curious cats to go in for a closer look. However, it is still important to never leave a baby and cat together unsupervised. Accidents can and do happen. Protect your precious baby and pet by supervising any time they spend together.

Myth 10: Cats cannot be trained.

This is simply not true. The trick to training a cat is understanding what motivates your cat and using it to your advantage. Part of the feline charm is that cats do what they want, when they want. You just have to find a way to make your cat think that she wants to do what you want her to do. You will not be able to order your cat to sit, fetch, and come when called. But if you build a relationship of mutual trust and respect, you will learn how your cat is motivated and how to use positive reinforcement to accomplish a great deal. (See chapter 6 for more about training your cat.)

Where Do Cats Come From?

The domestic cats you see on the street, in the pet store, and at your friend's house are members of the genus *Felis* and are called *Felis catus*. Other members of this nonroaring feline group include the cougar (*Felis concolor*), serval (*Felis serval*), lynx (*Felis lynx*), ocelot (*Felis paradalis*), and bobcat (*Felis rufus*). The roaring big cats make up the genus *Panthera*. This group includes the lion (*Panthera leo*), tiger (*Panthera tigris*), jaguar (*Panthera onca*), and leopard (*Panthera pardus*).

This Abyssinian cat resembles the African wildcat from which she descended.

Experts believe that our sweet-faced house cats likely descended from the African wildcat (*Felis silvestris libyca*), and genetic studies confirm this. These wildcats are small in size and are tan-colored, with tabby stripes and coat ticking similar to an Abyssinian cat's. If you stood a domestic cat next to her African cousin, it would be a challenge for you to pick out the wildcat.

Spend some time observing wildcats, and you will quickly recognize the similarities between them and your tiny pet. Resemblances include their astute hunting instincts, penchant for frequent catnaps, marking behaviors, and nocturnal preferences. Even the physical characteristics of shedding coats and retractable claws as well as the teeth, cheek muscles, and digestive systems of these shrewd, meat-eating hunters remain the same for small and big cats.

Domestic Blushing

Although scientists and historians have not pinpointed the exact date cats and humans became friends, historical evidence does show that cats and humans have a long history together. The first signs of domestication are from about 8,000 years ago on the island of Cyprus. It is likely that humans first tolerated cats because of their amazing hunting prowess; cats killed the mice and rats attracted to human food stores.

In about 4000 BC, cats joined the Egyptians in the Nile Delta, where an amazing relationship began. The Egyptians were the first people to actually leave records of their camaraderie with cats, and they immortalized cats in their writings and their art. What likely began as a working relationship blossomed into companionship and then worship by around 3000 BC. At this time, cats were fully domesticated and had graduated from simply an economic ally to a companion and house cat.

By 350 BC, cats were believed to be manifestations of the Egyptian goddess Bast (Bastet). This mother goddess had the body of a woman and the head of a cat. She was associated with fertility, grace, and beauty, and cats also received the Egyptian people's reverence and worship for their beauty, grace, and elegance.

Worldwide Respect

OTHER CULTURES ALSO REVERED THE CAT. THE ANCIENT Greeks associated cats with fertility and linked them to the moon goddess Artemis. Scandinavians associated the cat with Freyja, the goddess of the night. Muslims considered cats blessed creatures. There is evidence that Persians, Celtics, Chaldeans, and Medes also worshiped cats. Throughout history, cats have enjoyed a remarkable status in human culture while retaining their independence and the freedom to come and go at will.

Travels Abroad

By 1400 AD, cats were found throughout Europe and Asia. Thanks to trade, Phoenician merchants transported domesticated cats from Egypt to Europe, where cats continued to rid farmlands and homes of snakes and rodents.

During the medieval era in Europe, the cat's relationship with humans took a dramatic turn. Many religious groups associated cats with evil and witchcraft. Cats were persecuted and killed for this imaginary link with the devil. It's possible that the reduction of cats in Europe contributed to the spread of the plague during the Black Death in the mid-1300s. During this period, about half of the population of Europe died from this plague. Although uninformed humans were still trying to destroy

Your kitten is a natural hunter, and she will enjoy sharpening her skills by attacking toy mice, just as her ancestors cleared houses and farms of unwanted rodents.

cats, believing they were responsible for carrying and spreading the disease, these noble creatures were actually helping rid Europe of the disease-carrying rodents, thus reducing the number of plague outbreaks. This assistance helped increase the popularity of cats and eventually led to the end of their persecution.

Considered good luck aboard ships, cats continued their impeccable job as mousers and joined settlers in the New World. Domestic cats were imported from Europe to America in the mid-1700s to help deal with rodents that were threatening crops. These pioneer cats moved across the country with the settlers and soon established themselves as more than mousers and ratters in fields and barns. Pioneers added cats to their writings and paintings, demonstrating their status as companions. By the 1800s, cats could be found throughout the humanized world, and their popularity continued to rise.

Today's Feline Friends

Our house cats today share many of their wild cousins' traits, including the hunting behaviors of stalking, chasing, and pouncing as well as the territorial marking behaviors of scratching and spraying. However, cats have evolved from solitary hunters to fantastic family companions. Although their primary relationship with humans was more of a business arrangement—they were "hired" for vermin control—cats now enjoy a more social arrangement with humans.

Fans continue to admire cats for their beauty, grace, and elegance, but many also appreciate cats' independence and their individual personalities. Some cats continue to work at rodent and insect patrol, others seek stardom in the cat show world, and still others simply enjoy the domestic life.

This fluffy kitty has created a cozy bed and hideaway—inside an empty sewing basket!

2
Selecting
a Great Match

Kittens come in a variety of colors, shapes, and sizes. Choosing the best breed for you can be difficult, especially when the choices are as delightful as this trio.

W HEN IT COMES TO CHOOSING A FELINE COMPANION, it's imperative that you stop and think about what you want. Decisions based purely on emotion, compassion, or whim can have tragic results for you and your new pet. With an indoor-only lifestyle, quality care, and regular veterinary visits, cats often live into their late teens and early twenties. You are selecting a friend who will be around for a long time, so choose wisely.

Consider Your Lifestyle

How would you describe your family lifestyle? If your family spends most of the time outdoors or away from home, an active kitten will be bored; he is also likely to get into trouble if left alone in an empty house much of the day. You might want to consider bringing home two littermates or an adult with the kitten to help with training and to keep him company. Or you may want to rescue an adult cat who would enjoy the peace and quiet your lifestyle offers. For a family with a busy schedule, a cat or kitten who does not require daily grooming is also most appropriate.

Do you live alone or with others? If there are other people—whether adults or children—living with you, it's important to take their needs into consideration as you select your kitten friend. Make sure everyone in the home wants—or at the very least, accepts—your idea of getting a pet. No matter whose kitten he is, all household members will be affected. For example, people who suffer from pet allergies may not appreciate having a heavy-shedding cat invade their living space. The other people living with you must also be willing to keep dangerous items such as rubber bands, lit candles, and pieces of string away from the new kitten's access. If people in your household are home most of the day, make sure they want the company of a kitten as they go about their daily tasks. Take their wants and needs into consideration before bringing home any new pet.

Is your home quiet much of the day or full of activity? Certain breeds are more appropriate for busy or quiet environments. For example, the active and intelligent Oriental shorthair might be thrilled to live in a busy household where activity reigns. He can help "manage" everyone's activities both by vocalizing and by trotting along after everyone. The docile Persian, on the other hand, may be more suited for a calm, quiet household where the owners either are not around much of the day or prefer reading and relaxing to hustling and bustling.

Are there young children in the house? It's essential that you consider their maturity before bringing home a pet. For example,

Before bringing home that adorable kitten—or kittens, like these—carefully consider the impact having a kitten will have on your lifestyle.

toddlers are still learning muscle coordination and self-control. Without your commitment to always supervise interaction between the kitten and toddlers, accidents are likely to occur. However unintentional on the toddler's part, cornering or annoying a kitten will elicit a natural response from your kitten: biting or scratching to protect himself. And an unstable toddler, still learning how to stay balanced, can accidentally step or fall on your pet.

You'll also want a docile breed for homes with very young children who are still learning how to respect others and how to be gentle with smaller creatures. An assertive breed, such as a Siamese, may not tolerate the child's learning process as well as a docile breed would. Children and pets can enjoy a close and lasting relationship provided both parties' needs and abilities are addressed first.

Do you live in a studio apartment or in a large two-story home? Although cats often are ideal pets for smaller environments, they do need some space to exercise. And your kitten needs food and water bowls, a litter box, toys, and appropriate cat furniture on which to climb. In a small home or apartment, where space is at a premium, you'll need to be willing to make some sacrifices to provide for your kitten's needs. Sometimes smaller homes simply require a little more creativity on the owner's part: you can use vertical space when horizontal space is limited. But keep in mind that a small place may not be appropriate for a high-energy breed, such as a Bengal, who needs plenty of room for activity.

If you have a large home, you will probably have more choices as to where to store your kitten's things. And bringing home a pair of felines, along with all their supplies, is less likely to clutter a large home. You will need to provide playthings, water, and litter boxes on each floor of your home, however, so young kittens don't have too far to travel to satisfy their needs.

Do you travel a lot, or do you prefer spending time at home? If you travel often, you must arrange for someone to care for your kitten while you are away. You can board your pet at a veterinary or pet boarding facility, hire a professional pet sitter, or ask a friend or neighbor to feed your kitten, play with him, and clean his litter box while you are away. For homebodies, be prepared for your feline friend to incorporate your routine into his as he follows you around during some parts of the day and finds a good napping place during others.

These are important questions to ask yourself, as the answers to these questions help dictate the best type of cat to complement your lifestyle. All cats require time, but certain

This Cornish rex has extremely short hair—a plus if you don't want to spend much time with daily grooming!

breeds need more attention or grooming than others. Now is your chance to choose a breed that will fit into your lifestyle the best. The odds of your being happy increase when you carefully select the right cat for your lifestyle.

Check Your Budget

Make sure you're prepared for the expense of a new cat or kitten. When bringing home a healthy kitten, expect several veterinary visits the first year for vaccinations, spay or neuter surgery, and booster shots. A healthy adult cat who is fixed likely needs only annual veterinary checkups and dental cleanings. If you adopt a kitten with greater grooming needs than you are willing to maintain on your own, such as bathing, nail clipping, and combing out, be prepared for professional grooming visits each week or month, depending on your cat's needs. You'll also need to provide litter, boxes, food, toys, and other supplies. And don't forget that all animals carry the potential for unexpected illness or disease. Make sure that you have fully considered the financial implications before you purchase a pet.

List Your Wants

Before a tiny, purring angel steals your heart, decide what is important to you. Ask yourself, what do I want most in my companion cat? Few people are not infatuated with a tiny ball of fur, but every cuddly and playful kitten will mature into a cat with his own unique personality. Although your nurturing can affect your grown cat's personality, the nature of your kitten's breed will have a major impact on his final temperament. For example, your talkative Tonkinese is not likely to grow into a soft-spoken cat, and your placid Persian will probably never leap small buildings in a single bound. Consider activity level, grooming requirements, dependence versus independence, compatibility with other pets, meekness, need for attention, vocal tendencies, intelligence, and compatibility with children. Do you want a cat who will tell you about his day or a cat who will remain as active as a kitten throughout his adult years? Also make note if you prefer a certain look; perhaps you have always wanted a cat with all-black fur or one with a plumed tail like that of your childhood pet.

Do you currently have another pet to consider, or do you plan to add others during this new pet's lifetime? Bird owners must consider the added stress and reduced freedom their birds will experience with a cat in the home. Or perhaps your senior cat is really slowing down and sleeping a lot more. The energy and

This calm Persian kitten will probably stay pretty low-key and will require daily brushing.

friskiness of a young kitten might entertain your current cat—or it might drive him up a wall. If you plan to add a dog to the mix in a few years, you may be limited as to which canine breed you can select. Some breeds, such as hounds, naturally chase smaller animals and view them as prey. It's important to plan ahead when making a long-term commitment such as this one to your kitten.

Do a Little Research

To get an idea of what cat breeds are most compatible for you and your family, check out some magazines, books, and Web sites about purebred cats. This will give you a good idea about which breeds are the best fit for you and your family. For example, you'll learn that the Persian is a docile lap cat who requires frequent grooming to maintain his luxurious coat. You'll also learn that the Abyssinian has a short, low-maintenance coat and possesses seemingly boundless energy. The slender Siamese and Oriental breeds are likely to talk your ear off, but the sturdy Maine coon generally has much less to say.

The Breed for You at a Glance

HERE ARE SOME GENERAL POINTERS FOR HELPING YOU decide which breed is best for you:

- Lap Cats: Birman, exotic shorthair, Himalayan, Persian, ragdoll, Selkirk rex

- Active Breeds: Abyssinian, American curl, Balinese, Bengal, Burmese, colorpoint shorthair, Cornish rex, Devon rex, Egyptian mau, Japanese bobtail, Javanese, Korat, ocicat, Oriental, Siamese, Singapura, Somali, Sphynx, Tonkinese, Turkish Angora, Turkish van

- Heavy Hair Care: Himalayan, Persian

- Minimal Grooming: Abyssinian, American shorthair, American wirehair, Bengal, Bombay, British shorthair, Burmese, colorpoint shorthair, Cornish rex, Devon rex, Egyptian mau, exotic shorthair, Havana brown, Javanese, Korat, ocicat, Oriental, Russian blue, Siamese, Siberian, Singapura, Tonkinese

- Talkative: Balinese, colorpoint shorthair, Japanese bobtail, Javanese, Oriental, Siamese, Tonkinese

- Good with Children: American curl, American shorthair, Birman, Bombay, British shorthair, Cymric, exotic short hair, Himalayan, Maine coon, Manx, Persian, ragdoll, Siberian, sphynx

- Compatible with Other Pets: American curl, American short hair, Birman, Cymric, exotic shorthair, Himalayan, Maine coon, Manx, ocicat, Persian, ragdoll, Siberian, sphynx

Many people say their Maine coons are similar to dogs—affectionate and eager to be in the company of their owners.

This Manx is easily identifiable by his missing tail.

Indoors or Out?

The debate continues on whether cats should be kept indoors only, be allowed some outdoor access, or be permitted to come and go as they please. One thing is not debatable: research shows that indoor cats suffer fewer injuries and often live longer lives. My recommendation is to start your kitten off as an indoor-only animal right from the beginning. Of course, he'll want to experience the great outdoors; he's a curious kitten wanting to get to know the entire world. However, he also wants to eat your plants or play in the toilet, but you aren't going to allow those dangerous activities just because he wants to do them, right? (See chapter 6 for a more detailed discussion on outdoors versus indoors.)

Though some cats enjoy being outdoors, there are many risks associated with outside activities. He'll be safer if you keep him indoors from the beginning.

Decide How Many

Now that you have a clearer idea of what you're looking for, it's time to decide how many kittens you really want or need. If someone will be occupying your home most of the day and that person wants to interact with the kitten regularly, a single kitten will likely suffice. However, most people spend much of their days away from home, which can leave the family cat feeling quite lonely and bored. In this situation, it's wise to consider getting two cats or kittens so they can keep each other company when the human family members are out.

Kitten Pair

When it comes to bringing home a kitten, a pair is often worth the added expense and the initial challenge of training two frisky kittens instead of just one. Littermates are ideal because they're

If you decide you want two bundles of joy instead of one, consider choosing littermates. They have an established bond and can help each other adjust to their new home.

already friends, and they will help each other become used to you and to their new home. However, young kittens from different litters should bond easily. The two kittens will play together, groom one another, and share a treasured friendship. The social, behavioral, and psychological benefits the two will provide each other will be well worth the added cost.

Kitten and Adult Cat

Because kittens are so cute and tiny, adult cats are often more challenging to find homes for. By bringing an adult cat home, you'll have likely saved a life! You'll also have a built-in trainer to help your young kitten learn good behavior. With your helpful consistency, the older cat will naturally teach the kitten how to play nicely and help him learn litter box manners and other social skills. As with the kitten pair, the two will likely become quite bonded and will keep each other company when their human family is away. And most kittens are considered adults by two years of age (although a few breeds mature a little more slowly), so your cat will have another adult companion in fairly short order.

Adding to Existing Cats

When your home already includes a companion cat, the stakes are higher when choosing the right addition. Cats who are not used to animal companions can take longer finding a harmonious relationship with a new family pet. Choose a kitten who is more than six months old and is at least a year younger than your current cat. This age difference makes it easier for your older cat to maintain a more dominant role if he so chooses, and he can help teach the new youngster the ways of the house.

Although this may seem like a lot to think about in picking out a cute, cuddly feline companion, you want this long-term relationship to be the best one possible for everyone involved. Take your time and be fussy now; you don't want to commit to a relationship that doesn't work out in the end. With a little extra thought and planning, you will be able to bring home a new best friend!

CHAPTER

3

Finding
Your New Friend

Qualified breeders are reliable sources for finding happy, healthy kittens, such as these three Bengals. But animal shelters and rescue groups are two additional options.

N OW THAT YOU KNOW WHAT YOU ARE LOOKING FOR, where do you begin your search? There are several directions you can go to find your sweet new family member. A breeder or cattery provides pedigreed cats, and you can obtain purebred or mixed-breed cats through friends, neighbors, local ads, rescue groups, and shelters—and even from your own backyard if a stray or feral kitten finds you first!

Breeder

If you've decided on a specific breed, look for a caring, responsible breeder for your pedigreed kitten. Most breeders sincerely care about their cats and the integrity of the breeds. However, be an informed consumer. Unscrupulous people are out there, even in the cat fancy.

Attending a cat show gives you a perfect opportunity to meet multiple breeders and see their cats and kittens. Pick up a current issue of *Cat Fancy* magazine for a listing of upcoming cat shows in your area. If you have Internet access, visit the Web sites of some of the major cat registering associations that accept the breed you want, and locate a nearby show. (See the appendix for association contact information.) Take your time while walking around the show, and ask questions. When you meet with a breeder, find out how long that breeder has been in the cat fancy and what other cats he or she has bred. Ask about the person's cats and how they are raised. You can also find out if the breeder has any kittens currently available, when the next litter is expected, and whether there is a waiting list.

You can also contact cat clubs to obtain breeder member lists or contact cat registration associations for club and breeder

Once you've decided on a purebred—perhaps a Himalayan, like this kitten—take time to investigate breeders in your area.

member lists. (See the appendix.) Remember that each association has its own standards. Some overlap in their breed standards, and others include new or unique breeds. Keep in mind also that the term *purebred* has little meaning, as all domestic cats include some variety in their ancestry. What you're truly searching for is a pedigreed kitten—one with a traceable ancestry of several generations. This occurs when breeders register their cats when each new generation is born. With a pedigree, you can be certain that your kitten is part of a recognized breed. She can then be registered with any of the feline registering associations that accept her breed.

Here are ways for you to make sure you are dealing with a reputable breeder:

- Contact the cat registration association to which the breeder belongs. Find out about his or her credentials and experience. Look for someone with years (as opposed to months) of experience—someone who knows the breed very well.

- Call the breeder to ask questions. Prepare your list of questions before the call, and expect a caring breeder to ask some questions of you as well.

- Ask the breeder how the kittens are raised—underfoot with much access to human socialization, or isolated in a cattery? Kittens who are raised in a loving home and enjoy physical interaction with many people often make better pets as they're already comfortable with humans.

- Find out if you can schedule a visit to the cattery to see the environment for yourself and to meet prospective pet kittens in person. You'll want to see that the facility is clean and well furnished and that the animals seem clean and happy.

- Request a list of names and numbers of other owners with whom the breeder's cats have been placed. Contact these owners, and ask them about their experiences with the breeder and the cats. Ask about the cats' health and temperament and about the breeder's follow-up practices.

- Ask the breeder if the kitten has been to the veterinarian and which, if any, vaccines were administered. Write down the veterinarian's name and phone number so you can verify the information.

Read your contract thoroughly, and make sure you understand it completely. Caring breeders usually stipulate that you get your kitten spayed or neutered by a certain age and that they are willing to take the animal back if things don't work out between you and your new pet.

Local Advertisements, Friends, and Neighbors

At first, adopting a kitten through a "free to a good home" ad might seem to be an ideal option: no cost and you probably won't need to wait long to select and take home your new pet. However, keep in mind that things are not always what they seem. Although inexpensive in the beginning, your new pet might need vaccinations and spay or neuter surgery. She also could have an undetected illness.

To protect yourself, approach the owner in the same way you would a breeder. Ask questions about how the kitten was raised and why the owner needs to find her a new home. Check out the home for cleanliness, and ask to see the mama cat as well. How does she act? This may give you some idea of how your kitten may turn out.

If the kitten has received veterinary care, ask for the receipts so you know where she was taken, what vaccinations she has received, and what tests have been given to her. If the kitten has not received any veterinary care or testing, ask if the mother cat is current on her vaccinations and has tested negative for both feline leukemia virus (FeLV) and immunodeficiency virus (FIV). If not, you may end up with a very ill kitten and an unhappy ending.

Shelter or Rescue Adoption

Shelters and rescue organizations often have a selection of cats of all ages, personalities, and looks. Because of the large number of intact (not altered) cats out there, kittens are often available year-round. These cats are delightfully unpredictable because their breed—and therefore their temperament—is largely unknown.

Most of these rescue groups share the same goal: to find stable, loving, permanent homes for the cats and kittens in their care. You'll likely be asked to fill out adoption forms to answer questions about your home, family members (including other pets), and lifestyle. This is to ensure a good and permanent

These adorable kittens are two of the many available at animal shelters just waiting to be adopted.

Rescue Rewards

ADOPTING A KITTEN FROM A RESCUE GROUP CAN BE A *very rewarding experience for you and the kitten. Rescue groups often are made up of people who love animals and who dedicate their time and resources to helping save them. Some rescue groups are breed specific, and others simply rescue the cats and kittens who need it.*

When considering a rescued kitten, ask questions about the animal's background. For example, a kitten from a loving home whose owner has died or simply is no longer able to care for her may make an excellent pet for you. However, a kitten from an abusive situation will require more time and patience. You will need to retrain her to trust humans, and she may never regain complete trust. Find out if the kitten was relinquished because of behavior problems or other issues, and then ask how the kitten has been since living in her transitional home while awaiting adoption. An uneducated owner may not have understood what his or her pet was trying to communicate with certain behaviors and may have given up before really trying to correct the problem.

Most rescue groups want their animals to find permanent homes, so expect many questions from them and possibly even a home visit to make sure you and your kitten are a good match for a long relationship.

match. These groups also often offer post-adoption help with behavior training and socialization concerns.

Be sure to check out the facility, ask questions, and know what is required before you even look at the kittens. Some shelters require the adopted cat to live exclusively indoors, and some require an in-home visit before you can adopt. If you are not comfortable with any of their requirements, it's best to not have already invested your heart in a tiny ball of needy fur.

Most shelter and rescue kittens have received their initial vaccinations and treatment for any parasites they may have had. If your pet is not already fixed, there is probably a stipulation to do so in your adoption agreement. In the event that your shelter or rescue does not require spay or neuter surgery for your kitten, please do not add to the cat overpopulation problem—get your kitten fixed upon adoption or before she turns six months of age.

Stray Cats

If a kitten just shows up on your porch one day, you need to make sure she doesn't already belong to someone. The most obvious sign of ownership is a collar, with or without identification tags. If there is no collar, check for a microchip or tattooing. Microchip scanners are available at many shelters and veterinary clinics. While you're there, ask around to see if anyone has been searching for a lost pet matching your kitten's description. Check for lost kitten signs in your neighborhood as well.

Once you have determined that the kitten is ownerless, you must decide if you are willing to take on the care of a stray. You do not know whether her previous experiences with humans have been positive or negative, or if she has had any contact at all. (See the box on feral cats, those who have reverted to the wild.) If her experiences have been positive, she may acclimate to your home quickly and make a wonderful pet. If not, she may be frightened or aggressive or have behavior issues. You also will not know her health history—whether she has been vaccinated, or if she has any medical problems. Make sure you take a stray to the veterinarian for a complete checkup, including vaccinations and tests for common viruses and zoonoses (diseases that can be transferred from animal to human, such as ringworm) before she has access to

Stray kittens can make wonderful pets, but they need a thorough veterinary checkup to make sure they are free of diseases and parasites.

any of your current pets. She must remain isolated with limited human contact until after she is cleared by the veterinarian.

Veterinary Clinics

Pregnant cats or their unplanned litters may be left at veterinary clinics for many reasons. These clinics can also put you in touch with a client whose cat is expecting a litter and will be seeking good homes for the kittens. The benefit to you is that the veterinarian can verify where the kittens came from, the state of the mother cat's health, and the status of the kittens' vaccinations and health testing.

Some clinics also allow clients to put up ads for kittens they need to find homes for. Again, if you adopt your kitten using

Feral Cats

FOR ALL INTENTS AND PURPOSES, FERAL CATS ARE wild. They are no longer socialized to humans, if they ever were. Becoming the owner of a feral kitten is a complicated process; the kitten missed the early human handling and socialization necessary to teach her that humans can be friends. These kittens tend to remain wary of their owners and distant, and they have a hard time learning to live indoors and with other cats. Even a young feral kitten may already have distrust of humans ingrained in her. If you've decided to take in a feral cat or kitten in the neighborhood, contact a rescue group or shelter with experience in trapping feral cats; they can provide equipment, suggestions, and support during the long and challenging socialization process.

this method, you are more likely to get one with owners who value regular veterinary care for their pets, and you'll be more likely able to obtain the mama cat's and the kittens' health and vaccination histories.

Pet Stores

This section refers to pet stores that house and sell cats, often touted as pedigreed pets. Experts agree that prospective owners must use caution when choosing a potential pet kitten from a pet store. Do not confuse pet stores that sell pets with pet supply stores that allow shelters or rescues to bring in pets for adoption. The latter are excellent places to find kittens to adopt.

Designed for customer convenience, pet stores will not generally ask questions, as a breeder would, before selling you a kitten. Because stores may not know where the cats came from or how they were raised, you cannot be sure your kitten was

These three kittens appear to have lost their ears, but the folded ears give the breed its name: Scottish fold.

socialized unless the store staff works with the kittens regularly. There is normally no store follow-up or assistance with behavior training and socialization, so this is something you need to be mindful of.

Signs of a Healthy Kitten

When it's time to pick out your new friend, you must know what to look for. Start your relationship off on the right foot by choosing a healthy kitten. A healthy kitten is curious and playful. She should not cower from your hand nor struggle aggressively to escape your grasp. You also do not want a kitten who is excessively passive or unresponsive; she may be ill.

Look for bright eyes that do not run and a face without tear stains. The ears should be clean. If the kitten is shaking her head or scratching at her ears, she may be suffering from ear mites or an infection. The coat should be clean, soft, and glossy. Take a close look at the fur, and separate it while petting the kitten. If you see any black or red specks clinging to the cat's fur, she

Look for a healthy kitten like this one, with clear, bright eyes; clean ears; and a nose free of discharge.

probably has fleas. The kitten's nose should be clear, and you should not hear the kitten sneezing or wheezing; these can be signs of a respiratory problem or illness. Are the kitten's gums pink and teeth clean and white? The kitten's anus should be clean as well.

As you can see, no matter the direction you take to find your new kitten, it will require some knowledge and patience on your part. The likelihood of finding the right match for you, your family, and your lifestyle increases when you search for the best places to find your kitten and when you are willing to wait for the right kitten for you.

4

Welcome Home

Your kitten will appreciate having a nice bed and a variety of toys waiting for him when you bring him home.

You've selected the perfect feline friend. Now you must prepare to bring the little guy home. Responsible ownership means taking steps to ensure your new cat's safety and comfort.

Shopping Fun

It's very important that you buy basic pet supplies *before* bringing your kitten home. Bringing your kitten into a fully stocked room will make his transition smoother. Instead of being stressed when strange items are brought in, he can enjoy some peace and explore at will. If you haven't done so already, take a shopping trip. You can go to a pet supply store, a major chain store, or anywhere that sells cat supplies. Your basic needs list should include the items described in the following sections.

Kitty Furnishings

A carrier is necessary for bringing your kitten home, taking trips to the veterinarian (regular visits or emergencies), and traveling short distances. Options abound from inexpensive cardboard to hard plastic and from sturdy to soft-sided to fashion-forward. The important thing to consider is that the carrier is large enough for your cat or kitten to comfortably stand up and turn around inside. You can choose an appropriate size for your kitten and upgrade to a larger version as he grows or purchase an adult-size carrier right at the start. If you plan to do a lot of traveling with your pet, consider a larger crate with room for a small litter box for road trips.

This crate is perfect for its little occupant. It is sturdy but lightweight, and there is enough room for the kitten to grow.

You'll also need at least one litter box for your kitten. A simple, rectangular, plastic version is the typical starter box for most owners. Be sure the sides are low enough for your new pet to easily get inside. You can choose from a variety of colors, sizes, and designs, including covered or lidded boxes that offer your kitten some privacy and help keep the litter from flying out onto your floor; corner boxes you can hide neatly in the corner of any room; round boxes for a fun look and to keep urine and feces from getting stuck in the corners of the box; electronic boxes to reduce the amount of scooping you must actually do; and disposable boxes for traveling and for those who do not want to clean the litter box at all.

Some cats and kittens have a preference when it comes to covered or uncovered, and most find adjusting to an electronic litter box fairly simple, so the choice is largely yours. For an average-size, single-story home, one litter box per cat is fine. For two or more floors, provide a box on each floor to make it easier for your kitten to eliminate in the right place.

Along with your kitten's new litter box, you'll need filler, or litter. Stick with the same kind or one similar to what your kitten is already used to. This will reduce the number of adjustments your kitten must make during these early days. You can always try to switch your new pet to a different brand, formula, or material after he has adjusted to his new home. Go into any store that sells pet products, and you will find a plethora of litters to choose from.

The most common litter is clay, available in clumping and nonclumping formulas. Clay litter is designed to absorb moisture and help prevent odors, and some brands are less dusty than others and prevent tracking. *Clumping* simply means that the litter forms clumps around moisture so you can easily remove only the used litter mass and leave the rest in the box for future use. There are also litters made of recycled and natural materials such as newspaper, wheat, sawdust, and corn cob. These natural litters work similarly to clay but are biodegradable. If you prefer to flush the litter down your toilet, choose a flushable litter that is safe for septic and sewer systems. Recently, manufacturers have developed silica gel litter—in crystals or pearl shapes—that works like a sponge to absorb moisture. Most litter types also come in formulas and sizes for single-cat and multiple-cat households. You may need to experiment a bit to find the type of litter both you and your kitten can live with.

A convenient scoop for your kitten's litter box is essential. Cats appreciate a clean bathroom as much as you do. You'll need a sturdy litter scoop so you can clean his litter box each day. Most scoops are slotted and have a long handle that allows you to keep your hands far from the mess. Choose the style most comfortable to you as you'll be using this item at least once every day. Be sure the slots are large enough for clean litter to fall through but small enough to keep solids from returning to the box.

Another important piece of furniture is a scratching post. Scratching posts offer your kitten a proper outlet for his normal scratching behavior. Get your feline friend off on the right paw by providing at least one appropriate scratching spot. The post should have a sturdy base to prevent it from tipping over when your grown cat uses it. And make sure the post is tall enough for your new pet to get a full-body stretch. Texture options include carpeting, sisal rope, and bare logs. Avoid textures similar to those found elsewhere in your home to prevent confusion about what is acceptable to scratch.

Feeding Supplies

Your kitten will need at least two bowls, one for food and one for water. You'll find simple, colorful, and trendy styles in plastic, ceramic, stainless steel, and more. The preference is yours, provided your kitten can easily reach inside the bowls and you can clean them regularly. Check labels for dishwashing instructions, and be sure the glazes used on ceramic bowls are safe for food. Note that food oils linger on plastic dishes and can aggravate the skin condition in kittens who have feline acne.

Fountains are a popular option for cats' water needs and for those felines who prefer to drink moving water. You can always start with a water bowl and upgrade to a fountain a little later, after your kitten is comfortable in his new environment.

Your kitten needs a shallow bowl that makes it easy to access his food, and you will appreciate one that is dishwasher safe.

Obviously, your kitten will need food to eat. Not so obviously, you'll want to keep your new pet on the same diet he is used to eating. Unless the food is unhealthy for your kitten, it's best not to change his food until a later date, when his dietary needs change as he ages. Choose the right formula: kittens need more calories than adult cats do, overweight cats require fewer calories, and senior cats need specific nutrients to help them maintain good health. There are dry, semimoist, and canned food options available for cats of nearly every age and special need. Over time, if your kitten develops any health issues—from chronic hairballs to diabetes—he may need a special diet to help with his health. When the time comes, your veterinarian can help you decide on the best food for your precious kitten. (See chapter 6 for more on your kitten's diet.)

Day and Night Comforts

Cats love a soft, warm place to curl up in for a nap or to sleep. Buy a special bed or blanket for your new kitten. Options abound in this category as well. You can choose from flat, fuzzy mats to donut-shaped round beds to fashion-forward human-style beds. Warmth, comfort, and location are important for your kitten's bed. Some kittens prefer an enclosed style they can crawl into; others prefer to sprawl out on a pillow top. You may want to consider styles that have washable or easy-to-clean surfaces for your convenience as well.

Toys are a must for all cats and kittens. Small balls, crinkle toys, and toy mice are fun for batting around and chasing. Playgyms are larger pieces of furniture with dangling toys and various levels on which your kitten can leap, climb, and hang. Playgyms come in all shapes and sizes for climbing, scratching,

Everyone likes a comfy bed, and your kitten is no exception. This style offers a cozy nest for warmth, comfort, and a feeling of security.

and sometimes napping. Fishing pole–style toys offer opportunities for interactive play with you and your kitten. These toys usually have a fun object at the end of a string or cord that tempts your kitten to capture it.

Grooming Tools

Another essential item for your kitten is nail clippers. You can purchase clippers designed specifically for cats or use human nail clippers. Try both types to see which you prefer. (The specifics of how to trim your kitten's nails are covered in chapter 6.)

Although cats are notorious self-groomers, most enjoy being combed and brushed by their owners. Longhaired cats, in particular, need to be brushed weekly to keep their hair from matting. Regular brushing also helps reduce shedding in both long- and shorthaired breeds. A variety of brush styles and textures are available, including pin brushes with soft pins spaced

This Cornish rex is giving himself a thorough bath. Although your kitten will groom himself regularly, he will likely need to be brushed as well.

some distance apart (great for longhaired cats), slicker brushes with short and long pins spaced fairly closely together (ideal for shorthaired cats), and combs with wide to fine teeth. Ask the cat's breeder, your veterinarian, or a professional groomer for suggestions on the best choice for your kitten.

A flea comb is a fine-toothed metal comb designed for removing loose dander, dead skin cells, and shed hair, in addition to extracting fleas and flea dirt from your cat's coat. You can treat your kitten chemically for fleas at around six months of age, but consult your veterinarian before using any flea products on your young charge. And always follow the directions carefully.

Collars

Collars and identification tags are necessary for both indoor and outdoor cats for their safety. Choose from breakaway and regular collars in a variety of colors and materials. Breakaway styles help keep cats safe from strangulation or injury in case the collar catches on something; regular collars help cats keep their collar where it belongs around their necks. And ID tags are your kitten's best chance for being returned to you if he accidentally escapes from your home or gets lost while outside. On the tag, include at least your kitten's name and your telephone number, if not more information.

Extras

Beyond these necessities, you may want to invest in some extras as well. Cat or kitten treats are fun for you and your pet. They also can help you to lure your new kitten out of hiding, can provide a way to play, and are the perfect way to reward appropriate behaviors. Kittens can make mistakes, especially when placed in a new environment, so you may want to have some stain and odor remover on hand to tackle any messy elimination accidents,

Shopping List

MUSTS

- litter box
- litter
- scoop
- food
- food bowl
- water bowl or fountain
- bed
- brush
- flea comb
- nail clippers
- scratching post
- toys
- collar and ID tag
- carrier

Extras

treats, stain and odor remover, flea and tick control, heartworm preventative, dental care kit hairballs, spills, or vomit. If it's flea and tick season in your area, arm yourself with cat-specific flea and tick control. When using environmental treatments such as powders, foggers, or sprays, make sure they are safe for use around kittens, and follow the directions. Your veterinarian is an excellent source for product suggestions and to verify any safety concerns. Never use items on your cat that are not cat specific.

Check with your veterinarian for safe suggestions and to find out how soon you can begin using a heartworm preventative on your kitten. Heartworm disease is more common in dogs, but it is also a deadly—although easily preventable—disease in cats. And be aware that dental care is essential for your cat's long-term health. Begin to accustom your kitten to regular home dental care right away. Just a minute or two each day can protect your kitten from severe dental problems down the road. Use only cat-specific dental products on your pet, and don't hesitate to ask your veterinarian for a demonstration and advice.

The First Veterinary Visit

Schedule your kitten's first veterinary visit within the first week of bringing your sweet friend home. If you do not already have a veterinarian, check with family members, friends, neighbors, and co-workers for recommendations. You can also check with the place where you found your kitten or look up the American Animal Hospital Association or American Association of Feline Practitioners for providers. The veterinarian will be your partner in keeping your kitten healthy and happy, so choose carefully.

Bring a list of questions to ask your veterinarian. You'll want to find out what vaccinations are recommended, get answers to your behavior concerns, and obtain all the information

The Right Veterinarian for You

WHEN YOU VISIT THE FACILITY, KEEP SOME OF THESE questions in mind:

- Are there several veterinarians available in case your primary doctor is unavailable?
- Is there veterinary coverage after hours and throughout the weekend? If not, what emergency clinic do they recommend?
- Are appointments required?
- Are evening or weekend appointments available?
- Does the veterinarian appear to like and understand cats? This should be pretty obvious during the first visit.
- Is the veterinarian willing to answer your questions?

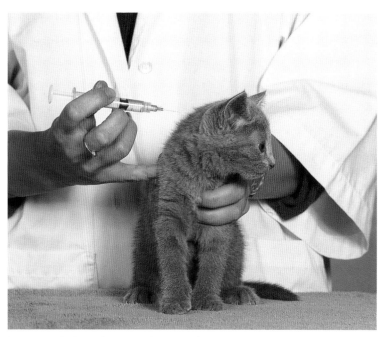

Be sure you find a vet before you bring your kitten home. This vet is feeling behind the kitten's leg for the right spot to give a vaccine.

you need to make educated decisions on your kitten's care and well-being. A qualified veterinarian should be able to help you with all dietary, behavioral, and medical questions you have concerning your kitten. (See chapter 6 for more on your kitten's veterinary visits.)

Cat Proof Your Home

Now that you have everything your new friend will need, it's essential that you prepare your home. The best method of kitten proofing your home is to follow the advice of experts: search your home from a cat's-eye view. Look for appealing cords to chew on, small areas to squeeze into and get stuck in, toxic plants to ingest, and fragile keepsakes to break. Although your cat is not out to destroy your home or kill himself, his curiosity and some of his natural behaviors (seeking high places, chewing when teething, and eating plants) may lead him down dangerous paths.

Danger Zones

Some of the most common household dangers include things you may never have thought about, from popular holiday plants to beautiful home accents. This section covers some important things for you to consider when it comes to keeping your kitten safe.

Most cats enjoy nibbling occasionally on grass and leaves. Unfortunately, many common houseplants are toxic to cats, causing illness and even death when ingested. Some common plant dangers include calla lilies, daffodils, Easter lilies, English ivy, irises, mistletoe, poinsettias, and tulips. Check the American Society for the Prevention of Cruelty to Animals' Web site at http://www.aspca.com for a list of toxic and nontoxic plants. Keep your plants and your pet safe by removing toxic plants or

Kittens are notorious for their curiosity and their ability to get into the most unlikely places, such as your luggage closet. (Travel, anyone?) For their safety—and your sanity—thoroughly cat proof your home.

keeping them inaccessible to your cat. Consider using silk or other plant options in your home as well.

Dangling cords are enticing items that can be especially attractive to young, teething kittens. Chewing on cords can cause accidental electric shock, fire, or damaged equipment. Keep cords inaccessible and unplugged when not in use. Consider using a cat-safe, bitter-tasting spray or rub on the cords to discourage your cat from putting these products in his mouth. Kittens can also accidentally strangle themselves in drapery pulls and similar cords, so keep them out of reach by using childproofing devices to wind them up.

Your curious kitten wants to explore his new home. He is likely to jump on tables, desks, bookcases, and more to investigate everything. This can result in his accidentally breaking some of your precious decorations and mementos. Some clever kittens even find pushing objects off shelves and tables to watch them fall to the floor a fascinating activity. Protect your belongings from accidental damage by keeping prized breakables packed away or out of your kitten's reach.

Tablecloths and drapery are lovely additions to any home, but they are equally enticing for curious kittens. Hanging fabrics create wonderful hiding and climbing places. Remove the temptation from unattended tables, and tie drapes back to reduce their appeal. Consider using pet-safe, double-sided tape that will not damage your fabrics but will discourage your kitten from playing with those items. It needn't be permanent and can help train your kitten that the tablecloth and drapes are not playthings.

The inside of a clothes dryer is considered a warm and comfy spot by many cats. This makes it a dangerous place for a

Be sure to teach your kitten not to climb your drapes, which could damage them and place the kitten in danger of falling.

nap. Eliminate the danger by always checking inside the dryer before turning it on and by keeping the door closed when the dryer is not in use.

You may be surprised at the tiny places your kitten can get himself into. Some common hiding places include under the bed, in a drawer, behind the bathtub, in a torn mattress lining, and in the fireplace. Do your best to block your kitten's access to potentially dangerous places such as behind the refrigerator, inside the walls or ceiling, and inside a recliner. For places that cannot be patched or blocked, remind family members to keep alert about where the kitten is located before closing the recliner, lighting the fire, or turning on the dryer.

Make sure all windows have securely fitting screens, complete with screen locks (which are inexpensive and easy to install). Cats often are fascinated with windows and the world outside. Countless cats and kittens have accidentally fallen outside the home by leaning or climbing on insecure, unlocked screens.

Bringing Kitten Home

The day has finally arrived, and your precious kitten is ready to come home with you. Make the transition smooth by being prepared and going slowly. You've made sure your home is safe and welcoming for the little one; now it's time to get his room all ready.

Set up your kitten's things in a spare room or bathroom where you can keep the door closed. This is your pet's safe room—a place to call his own as he adjusts to his new environment. Experts recommend giving your kitten his own space for the first few days to weeks (depending on how quickly he assimilates to your home). Place his litter box away from his bed and food and water bowls. This will keep flying litter out of your kitten's food and water, keeping them fresh longer. And who wants to eat right next to a bathroom, anyway? Keep interactive toys out of your cat's reach unless supervised. This will protect your kitten from becoming tied up in the toy and chewing through the cord or string.

To keep your kitten safe while bringing him home, put him in a crate. He will need to be in a crate any time he is traveling. He may not like it, but there should never be any exception to this rule. Cats instinctively seek out dark, warm places to hide when in uncomfortable situations, and a moving car and all the accompanying noises and smells can make for a very nervous kitten. The last thing you need as you drive is to have your kitten scale your shirt to jump into the back seat or hide under your car's brake pedal. And if you are in an accident, an uncrated kitten can be injured or can escape from the scene of the accident. To avoid these unpleasant situations, keep your kitten safely crated during any road trip, no matter how short.

Pets respond to the stress of travel in several very normal ways. Do not be alarmed or feel guilty if your kitten meows, lies silently curled in a ball at the back of the carrier, fights the carrier a bit trying to escape, or urinates and defecates in the carrier on the ride home. Some ways to calm your kitten include playing soft music, talking in a soothing voice, and remaining silent. Try all three to discover what your kitten responds to the most.

When you arrive home, immediately place your sweet pet in his safe room, and keep initial visits and visitors to a minimum. Nearly every smell and noise is completely new to your small friend. He needs some time to relax and get acquainted with his new surroundings. Simply place the carrier in the safe room, open the carrier door so your kitten can emerge when he's comfortable, and close the door to the room to give him some space. You need

A crate is the only safe way to transport your cat or kitten. Never leave home without one.

to curb your own excitement over your new pet, but you may sit quietly and calmly in the room with your kitten. Again, a typical feline reaction to all the newness is for the little guy to hide in a safe, dark place such as under a bed, inside the carrier, or in a closet. Let your kitten explore at his own pace.

If you have children, they must be quiet and considerate of their new family member. Closely supervise their brief meetings, and give the kitten plenty of time to himself. If you have other cats, separate them from your newest feline for at least a couple of weeks. All the cats need time to grow accustomed to each other's smells and presence without the added pressure of face-to-face confrontations.

As your pet relaxes in his new room, his curiosity will win out, and he'll begin to emerge from his hiding place to check out the new digs. Good signs to look for are your kitten eating his food, drinking his water, and using his litter box. Although your friend may not be ready to curl up in his new bed or play with you, he should show interest in consuming food and using the litter box in the first day or so.

For an extremely shy cat, you may need to move the food and water dishes close to his hiding place to ensure he will eat and drink something while remaining in his safe place. As is true for some people, some kittens take a little longer to feel comfortable in new surroundings. Stay positive, and give your kitten patience and understanding.

Reveling in Routine

Whether you live by your daily planner or hardly glance at the clock each day, your kitten needs a daily routine. These frisky critters thrive on a consistent schedule for eating, playing, and

Your kittens may be a little shy and apprehensive when they first arrive home. Give them some time alone in a safe spot until they are ready to explore on their own.

grooming, and these patterns help lessen your pet's daily stress. Owners everywhere remark on how their kittens will even remind them when it's time for a meal or some petting. Although you needn't become glued to the clock, attempt to schedule routine activities around the same time each day. Your newcomer may also appreciate it if you use similar patterns of words in a soothing voice during these activities. For example, when it's time for your kitten's playtime, you might always say, "Who wants to play?" Or you might consistently say, "Time for grooming" whenever you plan to brush your kitten.

Find something that works well for your family, and share the responsibilities with all the adults and older children. The litter box should be cleaned at least once a day, and you should completely wash the box and replace the litter weekly. You can feed your kitten anywhere from once each day to throughout the day. Timed feeders and free-feeding allow you some freedom with the dining routine. Check with your veterinarian for appropriate quantities for your kitten's particular needs.

If your pet spends most of his time home alone, it's important to have scheduled playtimes. Two or three 15-minute play sessions a day should be sufficient for healthy kittens. Daily grooming is required for certain breeds to keep their coats from matting. Grooming sessions also increase bonding with your pet and allow you to check for abnormalities on your kitten's body.

Some cats will add their own regular activities that coincide with the family routine. For example, my cat jumps onto my bed around 6:30 each morning for some petting and to curl up by my side until I get up for the day. He also meets me at the door when I get home from work each day. These are habits my cat initiated and has continued because I responded positively to the behaviors.

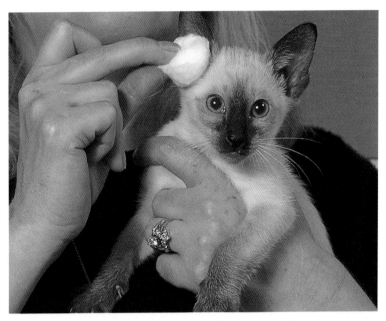

Daily grooming sessions are a great way to bond with your kitten and become alert to any potential health problems.

With some flexibility and effort, you and your kitten will establish a wonderful living arrangement together. It will not be long before a beautiful rhythm is established.

Meet the Family

During your kitten's early days in his new home, keep visitors to a minimum, and allow only one person at a time to enter the room. Each person should move slowly, speak softly, and never force the kitten to interact. Let your new pet make the first move. Keep other pets away from your new kitten as well. They all need time to get used to each other's smells and sounds before face-to-face confrontation.

As your kitten learns the new routine—feeding times, litter box cleaning times, play or visiting times—he will begin to meet you for these positive experiences. Start to use your kitten's name to get him accustomed to the sound; he will eventually learn and respond to it. You can also begin enticing your pet into interactive play by rolling a ball in the room or using a laser pointer.

When your kitten shows he is comfortable around you and you want to allow him access to the rest of your home, open the door to his room. But stay close by; until you are confident about your kitten's behavior around the home, supervise all free roaming. Confine other pets during these times of free roaming. Getting to know your home is something your kitten will do at his own pace, but he needs both supervision and space during these times.

Other Feline Friends

If you have additional cats in your home, you must use care and caution as they get to know each other. These are not relationships that can be forced. Older cats often accept kittens and eventually help care for and train them. But you cannot leave them alone together until you are sure they have accepted each other. They may become good friends, or they may only learn to cohabit; both are great accomplishments.

Begin introductions by rubbing both the cat and the kitten with the same towel to get both animals' scents on the towel. Let each cat have some time to investigate the other's scent on the towel. Feed them or offer them treats on either side of the safe room door so they incorporate the pleasurable act of eating with being around the other cat. Don't be alarmed if there is some hissing and growling between the cats. They are communicating with one another and determining their relationship.

In some households, there is an alpha cat who gets the most food, the highest perches, and other special treatment because of

These two felines are showing a little aggression. When introducing a new kitten to an established house cat, introduce them gradually and under close supervision.

his or her elevated rank. In other homes, the prime real estate or pecking order may rotate according to activity. For example, my cat Jack got to eat first; his littermate, Princess, always waited for him to finish before eating anything from her bowl. Tripper, only a year younger, often stole the top perch in our living room cat tree. Even if Princess was lying in the hammock, he would bother her until she moved; then he took the spot. In the bedroom, however, he took the lower perch, and the other two shared the top spot. Once in a while, I would find the three of them crammed together on the top of the bedroom perch. The three cats worked out their own hierarchy and got along well.

When your two cats become relaxed with each other's smells with the door between them, allow your new kitten to roam your resident cat's areas and allow the resident cat to check out the newcomer's space. Note that they should never be in the same place at the same time. Do not simply allow your resident cat to barge into the kitten's room while he is inside as this is an invasion of the kitten's territory and may encourage aggressive behavior.

As they continue to behave calmly toward each other's smells, you may allow some face-to-face interactions. Offer treats and verbal praise for appropriate behavior, and always supervise these meetings until you can be sure the cats will not harm each other. It can take as little as a day or as long as several months for the cats to become relaxed together. You'll need to show both cats lots of love, care, and affection to prevent them from becoming jealous of each other. As with everything else, patience on your part is essential. Finally, when your new kitten has acclimated to your home and both cats are able to be calm and perhaps even play or sleep together as friends, you can allow them to roam freely and interact without supervision.

Most cats will learn to get along eventually—if not becoming fast friends, at least tolerating each other and recognizing their place in the pecking order.

Canine Companions

Most dogs and cats can get along, but they may take longer to adjust to each other because of their extremely different makeup. As with cat-to-cat introductions, patience, rewards, and careful supervision are imperative. Both animals may be wary of each other, but they generally will not view each other as direct competition unless your dog notices a reduction in his attention from you.

Exchange scents between the two animals by using the towel as described above or by petting one after the other without washing your hands. Next, bring your leashed dog into a room and make him sit or lie down calmly. Allow your new kitten to enter at will. Keeping your dog as calm as possible will help smooth the introductions. There may be some hissing and barking at first as they check each other out. Keep these meetings brief and positive. Once the two animals are able to remain in the same room for longer periods of time and at closer proximities, you may begin to unleash the dog for short bouts. Both animals must remain calm and safe during these times.

As with feline friends, your kitten and dog may become buddies, or they may simply learn to tolerate one another and cohabit in your home. Consider either result a success.

Children

When introducing young children to your new kitten, do so gradually with a series of brief meetings. You must teach the children that your kitten is a sensitive, living creature and that if threatened or frightened, he may resort to scratching or biting for protection. Toddlers and young children should never interact with the cat unsupervised. They lack muscle control and don't know how to read the kitten's nonvocal and vocal cues, which

Cats and dogs aren't natural enemies, as this pair demonstrates. Just introduce them to each other gradually, keeping the dog on a leash and leaving the kitten an escape route.

can easily result in unpleasant or dangerous situations for the child or the kitten—or both.

For initial interactions, have your child sit quietly and calmly on the floor, and allow the kitten to approach on his own terms. Sit with your child, encourage the kitten to approach you,

How to Pick Up a Kitten

WHEN PICKING UP A CAT OR KITTEN, YOU MUST GIVE him a sense of security. This will help your pet learn to trust you and will reduce his initial inclination to escape from your grip. Place one hand underneath your kitten's chest, and hold his front legs gently but firmly. Cup your kitten's hindquarters with your other hand so he maintains a feeling of support while in the air. Holding your kitten close to your body with the same gentle firmness will increase his security and comfort in your arms. Don't fight with your kitten if he struggles to get away; just crouch low to the ground and release him. This will prevent injury to him from an accidental fall and scratches to you from his struggle.

This child has learned to hold her kitten properly, keeping the kitten close to her body and supporting the kitten's front and back legs.

and show your child how to gently pet the cat. Once your child shows consistent restraint and demonstrates a developing relationship with the kitten, you can teach the child to properly pick up and hold the kitten. It can take a while for people of any age to master this technique, so be patient and give the kitten time between tries so he doesn't fear letting the child pick him up and hold him.

An easy way to help your kitten and child relate is by using interactive toys and treats. Have your child toss a treat down the hall and share the joy of watching your frisky feline race for it. Teach your children how to tempt the kitten with a laser pointer on the ground and up the cat tree. Some cats love to fetch and may bring toy mice or balls back to the child for continued inter-action and play.

Remember that it can take anywhere from three weeks to four months for your kitten to completely adjust to his new home. Your patience and encouragement will go a long way toward achieving success.

5

Understanding the Feline Mind

Kittens love to explore, and they are programmed to stalk their "prey," as this little kitten is practicing.

Much of your kitten's behavior is based on her instincts. It's important for you and your family to remember that cats do not misbehave out of spite or to make trouble. They are following an instinct, responding to your reactions, or trying to communicate with you. By taking time to understand normal feline behaviors, you can eliminate some frustration and miscommunication between you and your new pet.

Nocturnal Madness

By nature, cats are nocturnal animals. They spend much of the day sleeping and use the quiet night to hunt and play. Your kitten is not trying to bug you when she leaps on your bed for playtime, calls to you from the hallway, or bounds through the house while the stars are still outside. She is inviting you to join in the normal nighttime fun. Thankfully, this is a behavior you can help to alter with a few basic guidelines (outlined in chapter 6). She just needs you to teach her that nighttime is not the appropriate time for interactive play.

Stalking and Pouncing

From your kitten's early playtimes with her littermates, her stalk and pounce behaviors began developing. How to kill prey is taught by the mama cat, but not all kittens learn this skill. Hunting and chasing are instinctual; your kitten was programmed from birth to chase, which helps her develop coordination and timing to capture prey, gauge distance, and make judgments through experience.

You cannot stop your pet from stalking and pouncing. This behavior will likely turn into mock-hunting play, discussed in more detail in chapter 7. If your kitten is allowed outside access on a harness and leash or in an enclosure, it is likely she will stalk accessible rodents, insects, and birds. Unfortunately, you cannot teach her not to kill birds or eliminate her natural hunting and chasing instincts. But keeping your kitten indoors will keep her from her potential prey and will likely lengthen her own life.

Scratching

Often one of the most frustrating of all feline behaviors, scratching is also one of the most misunderstood. Cats scratch for several reasons, none of which includes knowing that the sofa they chose is an antique or trying to show you who the boss is. Cats scratch as a way to condition their nails and help remove the dead sheaths. The act of scratching also fulfills a territorial

Make sure you offer your kitten plenty of appropriate scratching options, such as this triangular scratching post. Some kittens prefer sisal, whereas others prefer carpet, so a combination of materials may be the best approach.

instinct by leaving visible signs of claw marks and olfactory scent marks—pheromones, a form of chemical communication—that are detected only by other animals.

Similar to your practicing yoga, scratching helps your kitten exercise by stretching and working her muscles. Although aggravating for you, scratching is a healthy and normal instinctual behavior for your kitten. It is one you can learn to direct to an appropriate place (see chapter 6), but you cannot eliminate it.

Rubbing

There are scent glands that release pheromones located on your kitten's head and around her mouth. You'll notice her frequently rubbing these areas on items around your home including doorways, lamp shades, and even you. This type of territorial marking reflects a friendly social behavior, and it is often accompanied by purring. The act of rubbing means the people, pets, and household items being rubbed are all accepted into the family.

Sleeping Beauty

Cats typically sleep about sixteen hours a day, approximately two-thirds of their lives. This is completely normal and does not mean you have a lazy kitten. Whereas we generally lump our sleep time into one long event, cats break up their total sleep time into individual sessions throughout the day and night. You may find your friend taking a snooze several times each day in a variety of locations such as under the bed, in a sunny spot by a window, or on your lap as you read or watch television.

Kneading and Sucking

Also called making biscuits, kneading is a common, instinctual behavior your cat carries with her from birth. Newborn kittens knead on mama cat's belly while nursing to stimulate milk production. If weaned early, some kittens will continue sucking and kneading on human owners or on soft materials around the home, such as blankets, pillows, rugs, or clothes. Kneading is a pleasurable activity for your kitten and is often accompanied by purring. When your kitten kneads on you, she is also leaving her scent from the scent glands located on her paws.

You can almost hear these cats purring as they enjoy some mutual rubbing.

Spraying

Yuck! Unlike the subtle scent marks your kitten leaves when scratching, urine marking is strong and obvious. Unaltered males are extremely driven to mark their territory—your home—so get your male kitten neutered before he develops this habit. If challenged by another cat in or near the home, female cats and neutered males can also spray.

If you've never seen a male cat spray before, here's what to look for: The cat lifts his tail vertically and backs up to a surface. A small amount of urine appears in a fine spray from beneath the cat's tail. You'll also notice the tip of his tail quivering. When females spray, they generally do so from a squatting position.

To stop spraying behavior, you must find the reason behind it. If your male kitten is not fixed, schedule his neuter surgery now. If you've added a kitten to your resident cat's household, separate the two and slowly reintroduce them. Add a cat tree or gym to ensure there are enough perches for each cat or kitten to have his or her own space. If an outdoor cat is suddenly hanging around your property or antagonizing your kitten through the windows, your kitten's spraying can be more challenging to fix. Temporarily blocking your kitten's view of the outdoor cat until the cat finds a new home to visit may be your best and easiest solution. If need be, there are deterrent products available to discourage cats from entering your yard.

Wool Chewing

An animal's desire to eat nonfood materials is called pica. There are several theories as to why some kittens like to chew on wool and other materials. The more popular theories include early or abrupt weaning; dietary deficiencies; the relief of stress, anxiety, or boredom; and illnesses.

First, take your kitten to the veterinarian to make sure the reason behind her behavior is not medical. If it's not, attempt to deter your pet from these inappropriate food items by keeping them inaccessible or by applying a bitter or unpleasant tasting cat-safe product to them. See to it that your kitten has toys, perches, and a cat tree or gym to keep her occupied. Make sure you are spending time each day playing with and petting your kitten as well. If the behavior continues, your veterinarian or a feline behaviorist can offer additional tips and techniques to help you and your pet.

Excessive Vocalization

Not all cats vocalize, and some breeds are more likely to vocalize than others. Most owners learn to identify subtle nuances of their cat's vocabulary. Some of the noises include purring, answering to her name or recognizing something positive, calling to you, hissing or spitting when in a defensive position, chirping, chattering, growling, and silently meowing (the kitten's mouth opens but no sound comes out).

Some cats take their vocal communication to an extreme. This can drive even the most patient owner crazy, especially when your kitten decides to have these long, loud chats while you're trying to sleep. If you have an excessively vocal feline and you want her to give her motor mouth more of a break, try some of the techniques discussed in chapter 6.

Body Language

If you study cats in the wild, you don't usually hear them vocalizing to each other. These graceful creatures are masters of nonvocal communication. And if you're willing to observe, your kitten will teach you everything she's trying to say with her body. To help get you on your way, here is a beginner's guide to feline body language.

Take a look at your kitten's whiskers as she goes about her day. When she's just hanging out, perhaps during a bath or preparing for a nap, her whiskers are usually out to the sides and not spread out. But if something catches her eye and she is alert and ready for action, her whiskers turn forward and spread out. A fearful or irritated cat's whiskers flatten back against her face.

Easier to see from far away is your kitten's tail position. A relaxed cat holds her tail somewhat down, and some will tap the tip of it. An alert kitten's tail stands upright. A quick flick of her upright tail is like a greeting to say, "Hi," whereas a lashing or thumping tail reflects that the cat is irritated. As you've seen in pictures of traditional Halloween cats, a frightened or startled kitten puffs her tail out to make her look much bigger. Your kitten's tail will tell you a lot about what's going on in her head if you learn to pay attention. Of course, if you have a tailless or Manx cat, you won't observe this nonvocal tail communication, but these cats are no less able to communicate with their owners. Again, watch your cat throughout the day to learn these cues.

Ear position is another way to understand what your cat is saying. Watch how much your kitten's ears move, and notice all the positions they can take. The ears not only help your kitten understand the world around her but also help the world understand what's happening inside of her. When your kitten is in a friendly mood, you'll see her ears standing upright and a little forward. However, when she feels fearful or aggressive, her ears will flatten against her head and point down and back. Take the hint and back off.

This little kitten's tail and head are held up high, indicating that she is alert, interested, and ready to go.

A final mode of nonvocal communication is your kitten's body. Her posture provides a clear indication of her mood and feelings. A fearful kitten will often crouch down and sideways, facing the cause of her fear. You'll also see her hair puffed out to make her look as big as possible. When feeling relaxed and friendly, your kitten's hair will be smooth and her body position normal. When feeling affectionate, she may offer head bumps, rub against you, and share nose-to-nose touching. If her mood changes to playful, you'll find the addition of stalking movements, such as crouching down with rear in the air, hiding behind furniture, and pouncing on real or imagined objects. As mentioned above, aggressive kittens make their hair stand on end, creating the illusion that they are larger than they truly are. They either lie on their sides facing their opponents or face forward in a pouncing position, ready to either mount an attack or defend themselves.

Naughty Nature

It's important to your relationship with your kitten that you understand that cats do not demonstrate bad behavior. They are creatures of instinct and habit. What you may consider bad behaviors—getting on the table, begging for food, climbing the drapes—usually stem from instinct, boredom, or habits from a previous lifestyle.

Punishing your kitten is the worst thing you can do. Rather than changing the behavior, punishment often makes your pet afraid of you and possibly causes aggression because she feels threatened. Do not damage your relationship in this way. The next chapter offers excellent techniques to train your kitten to behave in appropriate ways.

CHAPTER

6

Healthy Habits

You may not be able to persuade these kittens to stay in this basket for long, but a little reward goes a long way in any training situation.

Y OUR KITTEN WILL DO AS NATURE AND HIS PAST experiences have taught him. And now that you have a basic understanding of where your kitten's behavior is coming from, it is time for your parenting to begin. By being consistent and patient, you can teach your kitten what is appropriate behavior in your home and begin building a lifelong relationship.

Behavior Training

When it comes to training a kitten, you must first understand what cats do naturally—as covered in the previous chapter—and what they respond to most: treats, praise, or affection. Every cat will respond to one or more of these rewards. Discover what your kitten prefers, and use it to help him learn and maintain good behaviors and change inappropriate habits. Basically, you want to reinforce or encourage your kitten's positive behaviors, such as scratching on his scratching post and staying off the table. You can reinforce his behavior in two ways: with positive reinforcement or with negative reinforcement, both of which are explained below.

Positive reinforcement is giving your kitten treats or praise for appropriate behaviors. For example, when your kitten scratches his scratching post, offer him a small treat or verbal and physical praise. By giving your kitten regular, positive rewards for his good behavior, you are encouraging him to repeat those behaviors; you are conditioning him to act in a certain way based on his desire for the affirming reward.

Negative reinforcement is using deterrents to discourage your kitten from certain behaviors. This should not be mistaken for punishment, an inhumane and ineffective method of training. An example of punishment is to smack your kitten when he jumps up on the table. Hitting your kitten will teach him several unfortunate things. First, he will learn to fear your hand and your presence. You may end up conditioning your new pet to cower or run away any time your hand or you approach him. It also reinforces that you are the reason for the consequence, not the behavior itself. If he knows that your hand is the means of punishment, he will simply avoid engaging in those behaviors in your presence.

An example of negative reinforcement is spritzing your kitten with water from a spray bottle or small water pistol when he jumps up on the table. The benefit of using negative reinforcement instead of smacking your kitten is that he will not necessarily make the connection that the spray of water comes from you, especially if you are clever about it. Your kitten will know that the water bottle or pistol is the punisher, not his new owner, and he will associate the behavior with the undesirable consequence of being spritzed.

Redirection is taking your kitten's focus off the undesirable behavior and moving it to something more fun and appropriate. For example, if your kitten loves attacking your feet as you make the bed, be prepared with some toy mice or balls to toss away from your feet. Most kittens will love the opportunity to chase any moving object, and the toy is just as good as your feet in your kitten's eyes.

Although it can be hard to avoid, do not become discouraged if your kitten does not end the inappropriate behaviors immediately. It will take time for him to realize that every time he jumps on the table he gets a spritz of water or a loud clap and

Redirecting your kitten's attention can be just as—or more—effective than rewarding or punishing him. Toys are a great distraction.

a firmly spoken "no." With your patience and steady training, your kitten will learn which behaviors earn positive rewards and which to avoid.

Not Like Dogs

YOU MUST ALSO REALIZE THAT CATS ARE NOT LIKE DOGS, who often will perform simply to please their owners. Although cats do want attention, affection, and approval, they want it on their own terms. Cats want to know, what's in it for me? So patience, consistency, and rewards are the best way to train your kitten.

Correcting Common Behavior Problems

Kittens are unique, and their early experiences and training can result in both good and bad behaviors. Your job as a loving new owner is to accept your new family member as he is and help him develop acceptable behaviors and reduce or eliminate unacceptable ones. No kitten comes without any behavior issues, but most are easily corrected with your loving guidance, patience, and consistency.

Experts say it takes about three weeks to break an old habit or form a new one, even for cats. The first few days are likely to be the hardest, but your persistence will pay off and lead to a more harmonious relationship between you and your kitten.

Inappropriate Elimination

One of the most common and frustrating problems owners encounter is inappropriate elimination: urinating or defecating outside the litter box. Kittens do not automatically use a litter box. You may have to spend some time training your young kitten if he has not already learned to use one. However, cats naturally prefer to eliminate in soft, sandlike textures and generally cover their deposits to keep predators from finding them. To begin training your young kitten, place him in the litter box and see what he does. You will probably see him sniffing and scratching around to begin with.

Some kittens are inspired to use their litter boxes immediately; others take more time. If your pet has an accident outside of the pan, clean it immediately, and place the remnants in the litter box to help him get the idea.

Cats of all ages can suddenly stop using the litter box. When they do, the reason often is illness. However, household stress, an unclean litter box, being threatened while using the box, or dislike of the litter can all result in inappropriate

Your kitten will most likely be litter box trained when you get him, but if not, it shouldn't take long for him to get the hang of it.

urination or avoiding the litter box. It's imperative for you to discover the reason and to fix it before the problem gets worse.

The first step is to take your cat to the veterinarian immediately because he may have a medical problem. Once that possibility is ruled out, take a closer look at the litter box. Is the pan located in a quiet, private, and low-traffic area? If not, try placing it somewhere more private. Have you recently switched litter brands or types? Another litter texture may be preferred. Are the sides low enough for the kitten to climb in easily? You may need another style of pan. Does your kitten scratch around in the litter or avoid touching it? If he balances on the side of the litter pan and refuses to put his paws on the litter, he clearly does not like the feel of the litter in his box. You'll want to find a different texture or brand. If your kitten is very particular, it may take a few tries to find a litter he really enjoys. Is the litter very fragrant? Cats are quite sensitive to smell, so the fragrance that helps you tolerate the litter box in your den may also be driving your kitten to use the living room carpet instead. Is there a new pet or person in the house? Is there a change in the routine? Changes in household members or routines can strongly affect your kitten.

Kittens are limited in ways they can express themselves, so elimination problems may be the first sign that something is not right. Try each solution one at a time until you isolate the problem. As you are testing each solution, you'll need to keep your kitten in his room unless supervised until you know he is using the litter box regularly again.

Scratching

Another challenging problem owners may face with their feline friends is inappropriate scratching. What many owners don't understand is that this behavior can be redirected with proper training and by offering the kittens alternatives. You are not going to get your kitten to stop scratching. This is an innate behavior he needs to perform. The key is for you to teach your kitten which household items are acceptable places to dig his claws into and which items to avoid.

Make sure your kitten has a couple of proper scratching products at his disposal. A basic corrugated cardboard scratcher with a toy of some sort (kittens don't generally respond to catnip when they're young, if ever) is a good horizontal option, or a traditional upright scratching post should do the trick. From the start, entice your kitten to play with and scratch on these items. Reward his good scratching with a treat and verbal praise. If he

Each time your kitten attempts to scratch an inappropriate item, such as your leather chair, place him on a scratching post so he connects the action of scratching with the proper place to do it.

tries to scratch something inappropriate—such as the carpet or a desk—use a stern tone when you say "no," and move the kitten to the scratcher or post. If you're patient and consistent, your kitten should get the idea after several tries.

As your kitten's freedom in your home grows, you must make sure appropriate scratching items are located throughout his territory and continue reinforcing the proper behavior. Consistency is the key to effective behavior training. If your kitten finds an inappropriate item that he just cannot resist scratching, make sure that proper items he does like are available in the same room. If the behavior persists, block his access to the inappropriate item for a week or two. If he still returns to the inappropriate scratching item, it's time to try some negative reinforcement.

Declawing

DECLAWING IS THE SURGICAL REMOVAL OF THE KITTEN'S front claws, and it's a drastic step to take to keep a cat from scratching. A controversial topic in the cat fancy, this procedure is performed under general anesthesia; the veterinarian amputates the kitten's first digit to remove the entire nail bed from the paw. You should consult with your veterinarian and thoroughly research the topic before deciding to have your kitten declawed.

A variety of products are available to help owners with this frustrating problem and avoid the drastic step of declawing. Depending on your price range and comfort level, you can find or make the perfect scratching deterrent for your kitten. Double-sided sticky tape can be applied to most surfaces and will keep cats from scratching because they do not like the sticky feeling on their paw pads. Vinyl nail caps can be placed over your kitten's nails to prevent damage when scratching, and they offer a great alternative to declawing. Motion detectors with alarms or that spray air can help keep cats out of certain areas and off tables. Pads that deliver a gentle static shock when touched also keep cats out of restricted rooms and off the furniture. Furniture covers protect your furniture from shed hair in addition to blocking Kitty's access to your favorite sofa cushions. Pheromone sprays help calm anxious kittens and can reduce their drive to scratch and mark the rug and other items around your home. You may even come up with some homemade alternatives, but check with your veterinarian for safety; the goal is behavior modification, not punishment.

It is very unlikely that the scratching problem will continue after you've tried the behavior modification options available. However, if the problem persists, consult your veterinarian, and consider looking for a certified feline behaviorist for additional suggestions.

Aggression

Most cases of aggression occur when the kitten is tired of being petted, in which case, he may bite you. The key is for you to learn to read your cat's nonvocal signals. The most obvious warning signs are dilated pupils and a twitching tail. Some cats also give a warning nip at the air, a smack with the paw, or a vocal sound. It's up to owners to learn the cues their cats offer and to respect those cues.

Cat-to-cat aggression can be an issue in some households. If your cats suddenly begin growling, hissing, and fighting with one another frequently, keep them separated unless you can supervise them. Create positive experiences between the cats by

Sometimes it's hard to tell playful nonverbal communication from aggression. This kitten is just batting playfully.

feeding them or offering them treats near each other. Try to discover what caused the fighting in the first place. Has something
changed in the cats' environment, your schedule, or outside the
home? Are there enough perches and levels for the cats to find
their own spaces? You may need to separate and reintroduce the
fighting cats (as described in chapter 4). A pheromone diffuser
may also help calm the cats and reduce their stress.

Excessive Vocalization

When a healthy cat begins vocalizing excessively, it usually
signals a medical problem or stress. If the vocalizing has suddenly
increased or occurs in similar situations each time—in the litter
box, after eating—your kitten may be trying to tell you about a
medical problem. Get your cat checked by the veterinarian right

away. Next, look for possible stressors in your kitten's environment. Again, have there been changes in your schedule, new additions to the household, or outside annoyances that may be affecting your kitten? Once you discover the reason for your kitten's jabber-jaws, you can work to reduce his stress. Hopefully, his vocalizing will be reduced as well.

Check your own behavior. Are you reinforcing the vocal behavior by positively responding to it each time? If you pet, offer treats to, or play with your kitten each time he talks to you, you're teaching him that he will get positive rewards for vocalizing to you. Even telling him to be quiet is giving him attention for the vocal behavior and can encourage it to continue. Instead, wait until your cat is quiet before feeding him or giving him what he is asking for. You can reduce his overvocalizing by making sure

Excessive vocalization can be annoying, and you may unintentionally reinforce it by responding, even negatively, to it.

you treat, pet, and play with your kitten enough each day, and try to do so when he has not come to you asking for it.

For middle-of-the-night vocalizing, try not responding to the talking. If that doesn't work after a few nights, you may want to ban him from your room or close him in a separate part of the house. Cats are smart, and they will get the message if you are consistent in what you are teaching them. If the problem continues, ask your veterinarian for some suggestions or for a referral to a feline behaviorist.

Veterinary Visits

As mentioned earlier, your kitten should visit the veterinarian as soon as possible after adoption and before interacting with any other pets in your home. Even if he appears healthy, you need to make sure he does not have any viruses that can be passed to other animals or to humans. No matter where you got your kitten and how healthy he's reported to be, get a second opinion from your own veterinarian.

Most cats do not like going to the veterinarian. Your kitten's behavior will probably be very uncharacteristic for him in this stressful and uncomfortable situation, so be prepared. Always use a carrier to transport your pet to and from the veterinary clinic, and leave him inside it while in the waiting room.

At this initial visit, bring as much information as possible, including your new pet's date of birth and vaccination records, if available. Make sure you tell your veterinarian everything you know about your kitten's history (medical and behavioral) and anything you have observed. This information will help the veterinarian determine if there are any potential concerns or if additional tests are needed.

Your kitten's physical exam will include taking his weight and temperature. The veterinarian will check your pet head to tail—including the mouth, ears, eyes, nose—and listen to the heart and lungs. During this exam, your veterinarian will be looking for any abnormal discharges or abscesses and checking internal organs.

Blood tests should also be performed. You want your kitten tested for common diseases such as feline leukemia virus (FeLV) and feline immunodeficiency virus (FIV). Although it sounds unpleasant, it's helpful for you to bring a small, fresh sample of your kitten's feces with you to the first visit. A one-quarter

Typical Vaccine Schedule for Kittens

THE AMERICAN ASSOCIATION OF FELINE PRACTITIONERS (AAFP) recommends the following core (C) vaccines for all kittens at the ages specified; the noncore (NC) vaccines should be given according to your veterinarian's recommendation and depending on your pet's lifestyle.

- 6 to 8 weeks: FRCP 3-way vaccine (C) for feline rhinotracheitis, calicivirus, and panleukopenia; or 4-way vaccine (NC) for feline rhinotracheitis, calicivirus, panleukopenia, and chlamydophilia felis
- 12 weeks: FRCP 3-way vaccine (C) booster or 4-way vaccine (NC) booster and FeLV vaccine (NC) for feline leukemia virus
- 16 weeks: Rabies vaccine (C), FeLV vaccine (NC) booster, and FIP vaccine (NC) for feline infectious peritonitis
- 20 weeks: FIP vaccine (NC) booster

Your kitten's vaccines are supplemented annually after twenty weeks of age. You can also ask your veterinarian about vaccines for bordetella, giardia, and feline immunodeficiency virus (FIV).

teaspoon sample in a plastic bag is sufficient. This will allow the veterinarian to test your kitten for internal parasites.

You will also want to ask the veterinarian for an appropriate vaccination schedule. Even indoor-only cats need certain vaccinations, and some states require them for all cats. The first set of vaccinations is usually given when kittens are about eight to ten weeks old. Vaccines help your kitten's body ward off certain viral and bacterial infections. They are an important part of your kitten's preventative health care, but the schedule should be decided based on your kitten's particular needs. Your veterinarian should explain how many visits are needed for the remaining vaccines and how far apart they should be administered.

Vaccine Risks

VACCINES CAN CAUSE REACTIONS, SO BE AWARE. MILD reactions include low-grade fever, joint discomfort, decreased appetite, injection site sensitivity, and reduced energy level. These symptoms generally show up within hours to days of the vaccination.

Anaphylactic shock is an uncommon but severe and potentially fatal allergic reaction. Symptoms include difficulty in breathing and a rapid heart rate. They usually appear within an hour of the vaccination and require immediate veterinary care.

A lump may develop at the injection site. If it does not resolve itself within a month, take your kitten back to the veterinarian. Some vaccines and injections have been linked to the development of fibrosarcomas (malignant tumors from fibrous connective tissue). To protect your kitten from fibrosarcomas, ask your veterinarian about nonsupplemented vaccines and alternative types such as intranasal (through the nose) or transdermal (topical application, such as a patch) vaccines.

Your veterinarian should also discuss your kitten's diet, grooming needs, flea-control options, and at-home dental care. This is also a good time to ask for a demonstration on proper nail trimming and grooming. Your veterinarian may also discuss spay or neuter surgery with you. Now is the time for you to decide when the surgery should be performed and express any concerns you may have about it. Kittens can be altered as early as age five or six weeks provided they can handle the anesthesia required, but veterinarians' policies differ. An overnight stay is not usually necessary for these simple procedures. Express all concerns to your veterinarian before the surgery, and do not hesitate to ask questions at any point in time.

Female cats are spayed. During this invasive surgery, the cat's ovaries and uterus are removed. The health benefits for female cats are that spaying keeps them from suffering the agonizing frustration during heat and prevents them from developing uterine and ovarian cancers. If performed before the kitten's first heat, spaying will also help prevent her from developing mammary tumors. The society's benefit is that you reduce the number of unwanted kittens in the world by preventing unwanted litters from your pet.

Male cats are neutered. This simple surgical procedure entails the removal of the cat's testicles. The surgery often results in a reduced roaming drive and helps curb aggressive behavior. Neutered males are less likely to spray, and the urine loses its strong marking scent.

At a minimum, your kitten needs annual visits to the veterinarian. These should include a checkup and vaccine boosters. You should also take your pet in when strange symptoms and behaviors crop up. Observation and education are vital when it

Checking your kitten's body every day for changes or abnormalities can allow you to identify problems before they become severe.

comes to staying on top of your kitten's health needs. Do not hesitate to take him to the veterinarian when you suspect something just isn't right.

Signs of Illness

Cats are masters at hiding illness; it's part of their survival instinct. It is your responsibility as your kitten's owner to be observant and alert to even subtle changes in his behavior. One way to keep an eye on your kitten's health is to give your kitten weekly miniphysicals—checking his body from nose to tail.

Upper respiratory infections (URIs) are the most common illnesses seen. Similar to humans' colds, URIs affect the kitten's nose, throat, and voice box. These infections can be caused by viruses or bacteria and are common in cats in large groups, as found in some catteries, animal shelters, and humane societies. Because these infections are transmitted through the air and are highly contagious, it is not surprising that new pets may show symptoms when first brought home. Symptoms include sneezing, coughing, a runny nose, and watery eyes. Isolate your ill kitten from other feline family members, and take him to the veterinarian to confirm diagnosis and receive antibiotics. You'll need to make sure your kitten continues to eat because his stuffed nose may reduce his ability to smell his food, and he may be reluctant to eat. Protect against dehydration as well by offering plenty of fresh water, administering it through an eyedropper if necessary.

Keep an eye out for these common signs of illness as well:

- **Change in Appetite:** Keep track of how much food and water your kitten normally consumes. This makes any changes in his appetite easier to detect. If you are free-feeding, you will need to measure how much you give and how much is left at the end of the day.

- **Lethargy:** Because your kitten normally sleeps so much, it can be challenging to notice whether he's sleeping more. Get to know his usual sleep patterns so you can tell when he's sleeping longer than usual. For example, if your kitten normally runs to meet you at the door when you return home from work, but he begins to take longer than usual or skips the greeting altogether several times in a row, this may indicate a problem.

- **Weight Loss:** It can take a while before you observe weight loss in your kitten, but by giving him weekly miniphysicals, you should notice if his ribs and backbone become more prominent. It's especially difficult to visually notice weight loss in longhaired kittens, but it's your responsibility to do so. Because of the animal's small size, the sudden loss of as little as one pound in a cat is reason for concern.

- **Change in Litter Box Habits:** If you notice your kitten visiting the litter box more frequently, straining without producing anything, crying during or after leaving the box, or eliminating outside the litter box, chances are he's suffering and needs veterinary care.

- **Vomiting:** Although it's perfectly normal for cats to occasionally cough or vomit up a hairball or food, it should not be a frequent occurrence. Consult your veterinarian if you notice an increase in vomiting frequency.

- **Change in Grooming Habits:** A decrease or increase in grooming may signal illness or stress. If your kitten's coat becomes quite oily and unkempt, he may be ill and unable to continue caring for himself. At the other extreme, if your kitten begins to groom himself excessively, he may develop an itchy or painful condition.

- **Aggression:** Sometimes cats who have a physical ailment become uncharacteristically aggressive toward humans or other pets. Do not put off a trip to the veterinarian when it comes to sudden aggression; this can be dangerous for you and other members of your household.

Lifestyle Choices

The most important thing you can give your kitten is a safe, healthy lifestyle. Experts recommend an indoor-only environment, but many cat owners believe that their cats cannot be truly happy without freedom to roam the outdoors. Although it is true that cats started out as wild creatures living outdoors, studies have found that cats do very well with a protected, indoor-only lifestyle, and they often live much longer, healthier lives. Additionally, if you look at your kitten's typical activities, an indoor-only lifestyle is ideal.

- **Sleep Cycle:** Cats spend most of their time sleeping. The outdoors is not required for your kitten to get in his snoozing hours. If he's looking for a sunny place, the sun coming in through a window will do just fine.

- **Grooming:** Your kitten can self-groom just as effectively on your kitchen floor as on your porch outside. But indoors, he is much less likely to be attacked by fleas, ticks, and other parasites.

- **Eating:** Manufacturers have developed a variety of nutritional options for your kitten and cat. You can tailor your indoor cat's diet to ensure he has the healthiest balance for whatever life stage he is in. He is also protected from accidentally eating poisoned or pesticide-laced meals or diseased animals.

This cat is content to snooze in his "treetop" bed, with no interest in the great outdoors beyond the window behind him.

- **Hunting and Playing:** These daily, stimulating activities are easily simulated in your home environment. Chapter 7 covers these outlets in greater detail, but cleverly placed cat treats, interactive toys, and the occasional fly or spider that manages to get inside your home easily replace the bird, lizard, or mouse an outdoor cat may find for entertainment.

- **Territory Patrol:** Your territorial pet will patrol your home with the same enthusiasm and possession he would have outside. The major difference is that he will not have to encounter predators, territorial or aggressive cats, and other dangers.

The average life span for outdoor cats is five years. In comparison, properly cared-for indoor cats often live into their late teens and early twenties. What an incredible difference! Cats who have never experienced the outdoors aren't likely to be

Common Outdoor Dangers

EVEN IF YOU'RE MONITORING HIS OUTDOOR ADVENTURES, you may not be able to prevent your kitten from coming into contact with these dangers:

- automobiles
- poisons, including pesticides and antifreeze
- fights with aggressive or territorial cats
- aggressive dogs
- abusive humans
- becoming lost or accidentally trapped
- exposure to a variety of diseases, including feline leukemia virus (FeLV), feline infectious peritonitis (FIP), feline immunodeficiency virus (FIV), and rabies
- predators, including coyotes and mountain lions
- contracting parasites such as fleas, roundworms, heartworms, and ticks

Harness Training

THE BEST WAY TO TRAIN YOUR KITTEN TO WALK ON A harness and leash is to start gradually.

1. Leave the harness out where your kitten can check it out and get used to the scent.
2. Next, put the harness on your pet for ten to fifteen minutes at a time. It will probably take your cat several days to get accustomed to the feel of the snug harness.
3. Attach the leash to the harness, and follow your kitten around with some gentle pulling. Do not allow the harness to drag behind your kitten as that may frighten him. Do not yank or pull on your kitten, or he may become reluctant to walk on the lead.
4. Be patient as your kitten gets used to the harness and leash. Make the first few times outside very short, and watch out for unleashed dogs while on your walk.

more than just curious about that great expanse beyond the doors and windows of their safe homes. And cats with previous outdoor experience can be converted to an indoor-only lifestyle with a little effort and consistency on their owner's part. You'll just need to be sure your kitten has adequate exercise outlets and daily playtimes to expend any pent-up energy and keep him from becoming a couch-potato cat.

With all the products manufacturers have developed to keep your pet entertained and your home still looking nice, outdoor access is an unnecessary part of life for your kitten. However, if you're not persuaded to keep your kitten indoors exclusively, there are two compromises you can consider: First, teach your pet to walk on a harness and leash. Yes, cats and kittens can learn to accept and even look forward to wearing the harness and being on a leash if they want to experience the outdoors enough. You will still have to protect your pet from poisons, parasites, and possible predators, but this way you can indulge your desire to give him time outside. Second, purchase or build an outdoor cat enclosure or enclosed porch. This compromise gives your kitten time out in the fresh air and sunshine while keeping him safe from predators, automobiles, and poisons. Make sure that the enclosure is secure and includes shaded areas so your kitten can escape from the sun as needed. Some climbing and resting pieces of furniture are great additions for your kitten's outdoor haven. He must have a place to keep warm in the winter and cool off in the summer, and you must still protect him from parasites, but this offers a nice option for you both.

Diet

As mentioned earlier, when you first bring your new kitten home, it's best to stick with his current diet. With all the changes he's going through, there is no need to send his digestive system into shock by changing his food. However, because of your kitten's unique needs, such as hairballs or activity level, you may want to choose a different diet with your veterinarian's help. You'll discuss diet changes at your kitten's annual exams, but you can ask your veterinarian at any time about your growing kitten's needs and whether it's time to change to a different formula.

Choosing a Good Diet

With all the formulas available, choosing the best diet for your kitten can be a challenge. Here are some guidelines:

- Do not feed your kitten dog food or other animal food. Cats have unique dietary needs, and feeding them a diet designed for a different animal can cause problems.

A good diet is essential to your pet's health. Choose a balanced diet and avoid overfeeding. A fat cat is an unhealthy cat.

- Unlike dogs, cats are strict carnivores. They require high-protein diets, amino acids, and other nutrients for good health. Your kitten needs extra minerals for strong bones, protein for growth, and calories to maintain his higher activity levels.

- Nutritional balance is essential for your kitten's current and future health. Give him the best chance for disease prevention and a long and healthy life by feeding your kitten a quality, balanced diet.

- Check the diet label to make sure the food meets guidelines established by the Association of American Feed Control Officials (AAFCO).

- Avoid feeding your kitten table scraps. Some foods can be harmful to cats, either because of the high amounts of fat, gristle, or bone fragments present or because the food itself is toxic. Onions and chocolate are just two examples of everyday foods that are toxic to cats.

- Feed your kitten according to the food manufacturer's guidelines and under your veterinarian's guidance. Overfeeding your kitten can cause obesity and increase his

Good-quality cat food is available in wet and dry formulations. Consult your veterinarian for assistance in choosing which is best for your kitten's unique needs.

chances of developing some dangerous diseases. By the same token, underfeeding your kitten can cause unhealthy weight loss and can open the door to additional health problems.

- Supplements are often unnecessary if you are feeding your kitten a balanced, AAFCO-approved diet. Too many of some kinds of vitamins or minerals can actually lead to toxicity. Always check with your veterinarian before adding anything to your pet's diet.

Dry or Canned?

Another decision you must make about your kitten's food is whether you offer dry or canned food. When it comes to nutrition, there is little difference between the two. And your kitten may already have developed a clear preference before he came home with you. Some benefits to dry food are convenience, less odor, and longer shelf life. However, canned food provides an

Not So Finicky

CATS ARE KNOWN AS FINICKY EATERS. HOWEVER, MOST *picky felines are made, not born. These creatures of habit often are quite happy eating the same brand of food their entire lives without complaint. Still, it's a good idea for you to slowly change your pet's diet every now and then. This way, if your kitten needs a special diet later in life, he will be more willing to try another brand or texture.*

additional source of liquid in case your kitten is prone to constipation or just doesn't drink as much water as he should.

Grooming Guide

Although cats are traditionally very clean animals—you're likely to find your kitten spending quite a bit of time each day grooming himself—you must help keep him in tip-top shape.

Nails

An important place to start your grooming tasks is with your kitten's sharp nails. Simply hold his tiny paw with a little pressure on the toe to make the claw extend out. Clip only the clear, white part; if you cut into the pink area (the quick), it will hurt your kitten. If you inadvertently clip the quick and your kitten's nail bleeds, use a cotton ball to hold pressure on the nail. The blood should clot in a few minutes. If it doesn't, use a styptic powder (available at most pet supply stores) to stop the bleeding.

You should trim the nails every week to two weeks, depending on how quickly they grow and sharpen. If they grow too long, the nails may pierce his paw pads—or human flesh.

Every few weeks, you'll need to trim your kitten's nails. He may object to this practice at first, but if you do it frequently, he will get used to the process.

The nails may also catch on carpet or clothing and possibly even be accidentally yanked out of his paw. Your veterinarian or a professional groomer can give you a trimming demonstration if you feel the need.

Coat

Brush and comb your shorthaired kitten's coat at least once a week and your longhaired kitten's coat every other day. Use a comb to get all the shedding out, and follow with a brush. This stimulates your kitten's skin and helps keep his coat clean and looking great. If you find mats, carefully comb them out. Do not try to cut the mat out if combing doesn't work; instead, take your kitten to a professional groomer or to your veterinarian.

A longhaired kitten like this one will need daily combing and brushing to remove all the shedding hair and to prevent the coat from matting.

Ears

When cleaning your kitten's delicate ears, gently wipe only the visible part of his ear, using a cotton ball and a cat-specific ear cleaner or a moist washcloth. Never clean inside your kitten's ear canal, as this can cause damage. Some kittens do such a great job of cleaning their ears they rarely, if ever, will need your assistance. However, some kittens may not be good at cleaning their ears thoroughly or may be prone to waxy buildup. Check for the brownish-colored wax visible in your kitten's ear, and you'll know when it's time for a cleaning. If you must clean them frequently (more than once a week), contact your veterinarian to see if there is a problem with your kitten's ears.

Not every kitten is adept at cleaning his own ears, so check them regularly to see if they need a little human help.

Eyes

Some breeds—especially those with very short noses, such as Persians—experience more tearing than others. If your cat is one of them, gently wipe his eyes with cat-safe eye wipes or a moist washcloth. Excessive tearing, called epiphora, can be caused by eye irritation and abnormal tear drainage. For eye irritations, visit the veterinarian to get the eye properly flushed out and ensure that the eye is clear and uninjured. Abnormal lacrimal lakes (where the tears collect after wetting the eyes) or nasal ducts (between the eye and nose where tears are carried into the nasal cavity) are the reasons for irregular tear drainage. Chronic excessive draining on the face can cause skin irritation, infection, and odor as well as stains from the tear pigments. Stains affect white-coated kittens the most because they are so easy to see. Take your kitten to the veterinarian or a veterinary ophthalmologist to find out how best to treat your kitten's epiphora.

Teeth

Dental hygiene affects not only your kitten's teeth and gums but also his overall health. Home dental care will help keep buildup of tartar and plaque (which appear as yellow and brown deposits on the teeth) from settling and causing major problems. Clean your kitten's teeth with a finger brush or gauze and a cat-specific toothpaste. Never use human toothpaste as cats are unable to spit it out, and it may be harmful to them if ingested. Pay particular attention to the gum line, where tartar often builds up. Although your kitten will probably not like the dental care, it should not

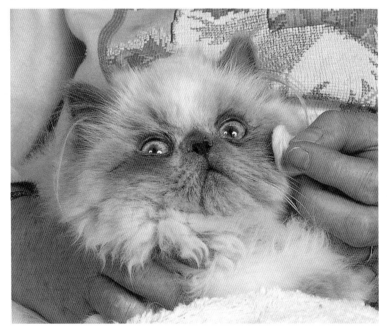

If you have a breed of kitten whose eyes tear frequently, you'll need to wipe his eyes regularly to prevent staining and skin irritation.

cause pain or bleeding. If either occurs, your kitten needs a trip to the veterinarian for medical treatment. Regular veterinary dental cleanings are recommended by the time your cat reaches about four years of age, unless a problem arises before then.

Bathing Beauties

MOST CATS, ESPECIALLY INDOOR-ONLY CATS, DO NOT need baths. However, if your kitten finds himself in a mess or needs to be bathed, use a cat-specific shampoo and lukewarm water from a gentle spray nozzle. Towel-dry your kitten, and then use a blow-dryer on a low setting. If you decide to take your kitten to a professional groomer, make sure the person has plenty of experience grooming cats and kittens.

Top Eight Emergencies

Despite your best precautions and watchful eye, accidents may still happen. The most important thing you can do in an emergency is to remain calm, know how to respond, and get your kitten to the veterinarian immediately.

Burns

Most kitten burns occur from objects such as heating pads, stove tops, heat lamps, or scalding liquids. For small, superficial burns, carefully apply cool water to the burn site to stop additional burning. Then apply a topical antibiotic cream to help with healing. For all other burns, immediately apply a cool, damp washcloth to the area. Do not put antiseptic ointments on the burn unless your veterinarian advises you to do so, as ointment may make matters worse. For superficial burns, apply an ice pack (never apply ice directly). Avoid putting cotton balls or batting on a burn because cotton particles can stick to the damaged skin.

Electric Shock

If your kitten manages to bite through an electrical cord, he will experience painful electric shock and burning of the mouth and tongue. In severe cases, the kitten may end up unconscious, go into cardiac arrest, develop pulmonary edema (an accumulation of fluid in the lungs), or even die. Do not touch your kitten if he is still touching the exposed electric wire. Unplug the cord, and use a dry stick (so you do not also become electrocuted) to move your kitten away from the wire. Then wrap your kitten in a towel, and take him to a veterinarian.

Choking

Curious kittens can easily get bones, string, or other objects stuck in their mouths or throats. If your kitten suddenly coughs or gasps, paws at his mouth, gags, or drools, he may be choking. Wrap your scared kitten in a towel, and have someone hold him while you look in his mouth for the object. You may need a flashlight. Never attempt to remove string, thread, or similar long, thin objects that may wrap through your kitten's internal system, as you can cause further damage; take the kitten to the veterinarian. Otherwise, try to remove the object with tweezers or needle-nose pliers. Be careful not to push the object farther back into the kitten's throat.

Heat Stroke

Most often caused by the unavailability of drinking water or being left in a poorly ventilated car exposed to the sun, heat stroke can cause brain damage or death. The symptoms of heat stroke include open-mouth breathing, panting, and drooling or foaming at the mouth. If your kitten demonstrates these symptoms, act quickly to reduce his body temperature. You can submerge him (except for his head, of course) in cool water or use a hose. Place ice packs around his head or neck, and get him to the veterinarian as quickly as possible.

Frostbite

Paw pads, ear tips, and tails are the body parts most likely to be affected by frostbite. This often occurs because an outdoor kitten is unable to find shelter from the extreme cold. You'll notice his skin go from pale to red and then become hot and painful to the touch. Swelling, peeling, and hair loss may also occur.

If your kitten experiences frostbite, get him to a warm area, and slowly begin to thaw his frostbitten body regions by applying warm, moist towels. Change the towels frequently, and discontinue warming once the frostbitten areas become flushed. Avoid rubbing or massaging frozen areas. When thawed, wrap your kitten in a blanket. Once the skin has thawed, you may safely apply antiseptic cream or petroleum jelly. Protect your kitten from further exposure to cold temperatures as the frostbitten areas may easily freeze again, and take him to the veterinarian.

Fractures

Kittens love to jump, and they're just learning to judge distances and balance, so bone fractures are common when they're young. The initial sign of a problem is either limping (favoring a leg) or using only three legs. You can apply a temporary splint made from a pencil, a tongue depressor, or a piece of heavy cardboard,

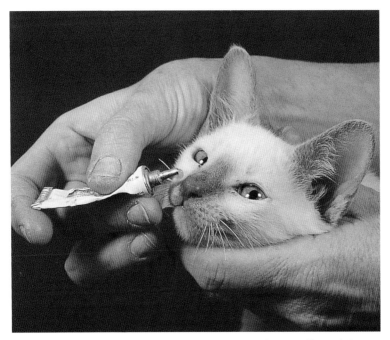

Your kitten may occasionally pick up a slight infection or suffer a small wound. You can treat these at home under the advice of a veterinarian.

held in place by strips of clean gauze or cloth to keep your kitten's leg from moving during your trip to the veterinary clinic.

Poisoning

Ingesting a toxic substance is the most common way cats are poisoned, but some items can be absorbed through your cat's skin. Prevention is the best way to protect your cat from accidental poisoning, so make sure all toxic substances are inaccessible to your cat. Here are some of the most common poisons:

- Cleaning supplies, including ammonia, bleach, and disinfectants
- Household items, such as mothballs, potpourri, nail polish remover, deodorant, and hair spray

- Car items, including gasoline, brake fluid, windshield wiper fluid, and antifreeze
- Snail or slug bait and other pesticides
- Human medicines, including acetaminophen, diet pills, laxatives, and rubbing alcohol
- Plants, including dieffenbachia, tulips (especially the bulbs), philodendron, and lilies
- Fumes from ammonia, carbon monoxide, and gas from cooking or heating

The general symptoms that might indicate that your cat ingested something poisonous include pain, nausea, and vomiting. Burns around the mouth can mean that your cat has swallowed something acidic. Never induce vomiting unless directed by a veterinarian; some chemicals are equally dangerous coming back up. Unless your veterinarian tells you otherwise, take your kitten to the clinic immediately.

Falls

Any time your kitten falls from a window, balcony, or bookcase, take him to the veterinarian for a checkup. Even if he isn't showing any visible signs of injury, he may have hairline fractures or internal trauma.

No matter how careful you are, accidents can and do happen. Be prepared. Keep your veterinarian's phone number handy, along with those of the local emergency clinic and the animal poison control hotline (listed in the resources section of the appendix). Have a well-stocked first aid kit on hand. Although your kit may help you deal with minor cuts and wounds, proper veterinary care is essential for your kitten's well-being. When a serious emergency occurs, remain calm and immediately take your kitten to a veterinarian.

For all major illnesses or injuries, rely on your veterinarian for expert care. If necessary, wrap your pet in a towel or blanket for warmth or to keep him immobile, and take him to the vet immediately.

First Aid Kit

VETERINARIANS RECOMMEND KEEPING A FIRST AID KIT *for pets handy to help you deal with household injuries. Your kit should include:*

- *adhesive tape*
- *styptic powder or pencil*
- *antibiotic ointment for eyes and skin*
- *magnifying glass*
- *cotton balls*
- *cotton-tipped swabs*
- *plastic or rubber gloves*
- *eyedropper*
- *flashlight*
- *rubbing alcohol*
- *gauze pads and roll*
- *hairball remedy*
- *hydrogen peroxide*
- *linen cloth, sheet, or blanket*
- *blunt-tipped scissors*
- *syringe*
- *teaspoon*
- *digital thermometer*
- *pair of tweezers or needle-nose pliers*

7

Positive
Play

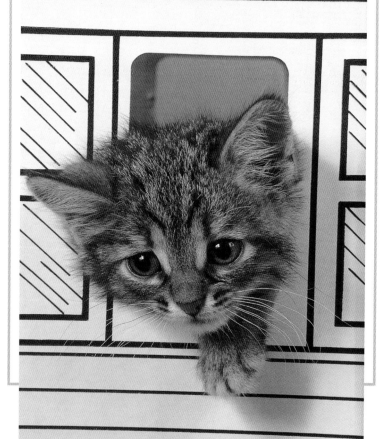

This hairless sphinx kitten is enjoying playtime in a combination scratching post and playgym.

YOU MAY BE SURPRISED TO LEARN THAT PLAYTIME IS essential to your kitten's health and well-being. Like her wild cousins, your kitten has predatory impulses—hunting and chasing—that must be exercised. While playing, your kitten will stalk and pounce on anything that moves as she perfects these predatory skills.

Play is also an exercise outlet to keep her in top physical condition as she works her muscles and improves her reflexes. Along with a good diet, regular play helps your kitten maintain a healthy weight. Although your frisky kitten may constantly seek out ways to burn off her endless energy, she may grow a little lazy as she gets older. Starting daily play and exercise sessions now will establish a good routine for you both as your kitten ages.

Play Ways

There are two basic styles of play for cats: social and solo. Both are important for stimulating your kitten's senses and helping her maintain a healthy body condition.

As the name implies, solo play is an activity your kitten does on her own. Balls, catnip mice, and stand-alone toys with springing or swinging targets all make good individual games for your kitten. When you're away from home or sleeping at night, leave these types of independent play toys around for your kitten to entertain herself with. Just make sure they have no small parts that can be chewed or pulled off (choking hazard) or string your kitten could ingest or strangle herself with.

Interactive games allow you to play with your cat and deepen your bond together. They also teach your kitten what

Like this playful Bengal, your kitten will probably spend hours playing by herself with a few simple toys. And she'll gladly chase after thrown balls.

behavior is and is not appropriate for play, such as biting. Fishing pole toys with feathers or catnip-filled objects on the ends, handheld wands, laser pointers, catnip bubbles, and toys to toss (you can use solitary toys for this) are ideal for social play with your kitten.

Rules of Engagement

To protect yourself and your kitten, it's important for you to make and enforce boundaries. Following are some important dos and don'ts when it comes to playing with your kitten.

Don't play with her the same way you would play with a puppy. Although some cats will play fetch and will walk on a leash, realize now that your kitten is not a low-maintenance dog. She's not going to want to wrestle with you, play roughly, or indulge you in a tug of war with a chew toy. She is a different species with her own needs, personality, and motivation. Learn all you can about your new pet, and be willing to play her way.

Do play with your kitten every day. Establish the habit when your kitten is young and your relationship is just beginning. Just fifteen to twenty minutes, two or three times a day, will make a huge difference for you and your kitten. If your kitten will be spending much of the day alone, scheduling a play session before work, in the evening, and before you go to bed for the night will keep your kitten entertained and help wear her out before you go to sleep.

Don't use your fingers to play with your kitten. Although her bites may be cute and a minor annoyance now, a bite from her adult teeth will be painful. You also don't want to teach your kitten that it's acceptable to bite people. Begin teaching her now that biting is never acceptable, not even during play.

Do set limits and stick to them. If your kitten bites you, say "no" and end the game immediately. If she attacks you when you're not playing, say "no" and spritz her with water or walk away.

Don't force your kitten to play when she's not in the mood. Part of social play with your kitten requires you to pay attention to her limits. If she's in the middle of a self-grooming session, if she's taking a nap, or even if she just seems grumpy, it's not a good time for a play session. If you notice your kitten becoming overstimulated during play, take a break. This will reduce your chances of getting nipped or scratched.

Do learn to play in ways that increase your kitten's confidence, entertainment, and enthusiasm. When playing with your kitten, it's important to allow her to catch her "prey" sometimes so she does not become discouraged and stop trying. Reward your kitten with a treat or meal after playtime. In the wild, she would be rewarded for capturing her prey with some food.

Don't exhaust your kitten. Playtime is not meant to be a marathon exercise session but rather a fun and healthy activity. Allow for mental and physical stimulation.

Do reward positive play to encourage her to continue that appropriate behavior. When she's playing with proper objects, continue the play and offer treats and reinforcement. This is behavior you want to last.

Tempting Techniques

When it comes to interactive play, it probably won't take much to get your kitten engaged. Cats are born with the natural desire to stalk and pounce on anything that moves. The trick is to establish regular times for you to play with your kitten and discover how your kitten most likes to play. Simple movements

Be sure to let your kitten dictate how long your play sessions last, and don't force her into play if she's otherwise engaged.

should distract your kitten from thinking about her next meal or nap and get her mind and body active.

Feathered Fun: When using feathered toys, try to imitate the flight of real birds. Add frequent "landings" on appropriate places for your cat to pounce on. Keep the speed and transitions realistic to keep your kitten interested and appropriately mentally and physically challenged.

Mice Madness: Mice are a favorite prey for many cats, and your best bet is to hide or toss these around your home. For additional fun, choose mice laced with catnip, mice on a string, or battery-operated mice.

Tempting Teasers: Designed to resemble a snake or reptile, teasers can be dragged along the ground, swiveled, and

Toys that move on their own at the slightest touch generally fascinate kittens and encourage them to play. This little kitten seems a bit leery of this elaborate plaything, but soon she'll give it a try.

shaken to imitate real cold-blooded prey. Incorporate frequent freezes in action, as reptiles might do in the wild.

Ball Bonanza: Simple toys, such as Ping-Pong balls and other lightweight balls, provide excellent stimulation for cats of all ages. Roll one down the hall, or hide them in your home for your kitten to find when you're at work or asleep. Each time your kitten swats at the ball, it moves away for your kitten to chase as she would a prey. Treat- or kibble-dispensing balls offer your kitten the food reward.

Lively Lasers: Trail the beam across the floor and up the cat tree. Your frisky kitten's sure to follow at warp speed. Laser pointers require the least amount of effort for you and tempt most felines to get up and play. Because your kitten does not get to really catch anything with these toys, be sure to properly reward her at the end of laser play.

Bond with Baby

Engaging in active playtime with your kitten helps her bond to you and become more comfortable with her new home. It gives her a chance to exercise, build confidence, and get rid of pent-up energy or stress. You can look forward to watching your tiny friend develop and sharpen her skills and witnessing her personality emerge. She, in turn, will look forward to enjoying positive experiences with her delightful new owner, and she will become even more attached to you.

Your kitten will always find ways to spend her time. The key during these early days of your relationship is to teach her what are appropriate activities and what is not allowed in your home. In addition to training her, you're solidifying your relationship by spending time together just having fun.

Dangerous Toys

AVOID THESE TOYS, AS THEY CAN CAUSE CHOKING OR internal blockages if ingested:

plastic bags	buttons
ribbon	bells
string	rubber bands
dental floss	plastic rings from milk
aluminum foil	or juice containers

8

Show
Primer

This pretty kitten appears primed for the show ring. You may want to show off your pet or just watch the competition; a cat show has something for every cat fancier.

JUST IMAGINE A LARGE HALL, THE BUZZ OF EXCITEMENT, row upon row of decorated cages, and some of the most beautiful cats and kittens you've ever seen. Their coats are groomed to perfection, and ribbons adorn the cages of that day's winners. Cat shows are filled with a variety of pedigreed and household cats and kittens, cat paraphernalia, judging rings, and education for everyone. Proud owners are often thrilled to tell you about their prized cats. If you've never attended a cat show before, it's an amazing experience. And you might just get hooked!

Join in the Fun

Most shows are for pedigreed cats or kittens only. Some specialty shows focus on certain hair lengths or breeds. All-breed shows feature all recognized breeds within that association. Some are restricted to pedigreed cats, whereas others allow household pets to compete as well. Cats do not perform at these shows, although their personalities definitely shine through as judges evaluate them. Instead, cats and kittens are judged on how closely they match their breed's standard description, from overall size, coat color, and ear shape to tail length, bone structure, and distance between their eyes.

To get involved in showing your cat or kitten, check with the registration association(s) with which your kitten is registered. Obtain a copy of their show rules and the breed standard for your breed of cat. By studying the breed standard and what that association considers disqualifying features for showing your breed, you can get a better idea of whether your kitten qualifies for the pedigreed competitions or whether you should show him in a household pet category. (Most shows offer household pet categories, and cats needn't be registered to be shown.)

Visit a couple of shows as a spectator. Observe and talk to competitors at these shows to learn what to expect and to familiarize yourself with the many activities that take place at cat shows. For a list of shows in your area, check the cat registration association's Web site, read the latest issue of *Cat Fancy* magazine, or contact a local cat club.

To compete in a show, you must contact the entry clerk and fill out an entry form for each cat or kitten you want to enter in the show. Your pets must be registered, vaccinated, and healthy. Most associations do not allow declawed cats to compete. And there are entry fees for competition.

See if your association has a mentor program. If so, this can be a great help for newcomers to the cat show world. In a typical

Before you pack up for the show, give your kitten a thorough grooming. You can touch him up with a comb and brush at the show, but nail clipping should definitely be done in advance.

mentor program, you will be teamed up with a show veteran who can assist you with show etiquette, provide tips, and help you understand the show in general.

Plan Ahead, Be Prepared

Be sure to allow extra travel time in case something unexpected occurs on the way to the show hall, such as encountering heavy traffic or getting lost. Experts recommend arriving at the show hall an hour before the actual judging begins. Then you'll check in with the entry clerk, who will give you your cage number and benching row designation. (This tells you where your cage will be kept during the show.)

Make sure you have everything you need:

- **Cage:** Size allowances are listed on the show announcement you receive when processing entry paperwork and payment. Most shows provide the basic wire cages, but check beforehand.

- **Curtains and Clips:** Usually made of a sturdy piece of material cut to line the inside or outside of the cat's cage, these curtains prevent your cat from seeing his feline neighbors and help reduce quarrels between cats. Consider selecting a curtain color that will accentuate your cat's or kitten's appearance. Experts recommend choosing an easy-to-clean material. At a show, you'll see everything from plain and simple to extravagant cage setups.

- **Litter and Pan:** Although many shows provide litter, it's a good idea to bring a litter and pan your pet is already comfortable with. Several manufacturers offer disposable and travel litter boxes with litter and scoop, which may be perfect for your show needs.

- **Food and Water:** Expect to be at the show all day (typically 9 a.m. to 4 p.m.), which means your cat or kitten will need food and plenty of clean water for the duration. Some shows provide food, but again, you know what your cat likes, and most experts recommend bringing your animal's favorite food for the show. If your pet is nervous, he may not eat during the show, but offer the food anyway. Either way, he will likely devour his food once he returns home.

- **Cozy Bed or Hammock:** Your cat or kitten will need a comfy place for naps throughout the day. Again, choose easy-to-wash materials.

- **Toys and Treats:** Bring a couple of toys and favorite treats for play and rewards throughout the day.

- **Grooming Supplies:** As this is a cat show, your friend's appearance will be judged, so grooming supplies are essential. A comb (especially for longhaired cats) or brush (best for shorthaired cats) is necessary. Combs will also help remove any litter or elimination accidents from your pet's rear end. Claws should already be clipped, so clippers are not necessary. Wipes for your kitten's eyes are useful.

- **Confirmation Slip:** Bring the slip you received from the entry clerk when you registered.

- **Vaccination Records:** Your cat(s) or kitten(s) must be healthy and current on vaccinations. Bring proof, just in case you need it.

- **Comfort for You:** Consider bringing your own lunch, drinks, and snacks. Although vendors probably will be selling food at most halls, the prices are usually high. A pen and index or note cards are useful for notes, questions, and signage. Experts also recommend lining the cage bottom with newspaper, carpet samples, or paper bags. And bring a bag for disposing of your own trash to keep your area tidy and prevent having to frequently search for public trash receptacles. A book or friend can also help pass the time when you are waiting for your next ring judging. There is a lot of time between judgings.

Once you locate your cage assignment, make your cat or kitten comfortable, and take a tour around the judging rings. The

Bring some of your kitten's favorite food to the show. He may be too stimulated to eat, but you should have it on hand in case he gets hungry.

rings are generally located together in a group with curtains separating them. In each ring, you'll find several cages in a U shape, a judging table, and chairs for the audience. Each ring lists the judge's name and the schedule for the ring. Check the judging schedule (write it down if you need to), and make sure you know where each ring is located so you don't arrive late or completely miss your pet's judging.

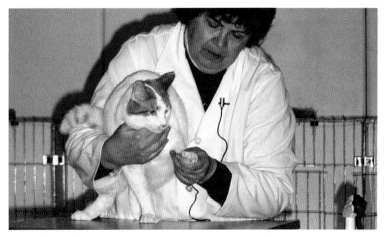

At the show, the judge will examine every cat and kitten carefully, measuring them against the breed's standards.

Basic Categories

Each registration association has its own titles. In general, there are three show classifications: Nonchampionship, Championship, and Alter or Premiership.

Under Nonchampionship classes, you'll find five divisions. Kitten Class is for four- to eight-month-old pedigreed kittens. Any Other Variety (AOV) Class is for unaltered, pedigreed cats or kittens who qualify for Championship or Alter competition but do not conform to the association's standard in color or coat. Provisional Breed Class is for unaltered, pedigreed cats (eight months or older by the first day of the show) who are not currently accepted for Championship competition. Miscellaneous Class is for breeds who are not yet accepted for Provisional Breed competition but are accepted for registration. Household Pet Class (HHP) is an opportunity for nonpedigreed cats and pedigreed cats with a disqualifying trait (according to the breed standard) to compete.

In the Championship classes, there are three divisions: Open Class is for unaltered, pedigreed cats who have not achieved championship status; requirements for championship status differ with each registration association. Champion Class is for unaltered, pedigreed cats who have received champion status. Grand Champion Class is for unaltered, pedigreed cats who have attained grand champion status, which has different requirements depending on the registration association.

The Alter or Premiership classes are for spayed and neutered (altered) cats who would be eligible for Championship if they were not altered.

In each show, the judges select the Best of Color or Breed for the cats who best exemplify their breeds' physical look; and the Best of Show, for the most beautiful cat for the entire show. In the show Final, the big moment for show contestants, the judge will present rosettes to the top five to ten cats.

Understanding the Show

Throughout the show hall, several separate, concurrent shows occur in each judging ring. There are usually six to eight rings. Judges are knowledgeable people who have bred, shown, and championed several cat breeds, in addition to having served at many positions at shows; some associations require that judges pass written exams. These people are extremely educated about the cat fancy.

When your kitten's number is called, you will take him to the appropriate ring, place him in the judging cage that shows your kitten's number on it, secure the cage door, and leave the ring. Once the judge has evaluated each kitten in the competition, he or she will place appropriate ribbons on the cages, announcing the winners for that particular show. When the judge or clerk dismisses the kittens, you will get your kitten and ribbon(s) and return to your benching cage until your kitten's number is called for the next judging ring on your schedule.

Mind Your Manners

Whether you are an exhibitor or an attendee, there are certain rules of etiquette you should observe when attending a cat show. Always ask for permission before touching a cat or kitten. Exhibitors have spent much time and energy grooming their cats for these shows, and spreading germs is a major concern. Although the cats must be in top health and vaccinated to even attend the show, germs still exist and are easily spread by petting one cat, then another, then another. Finally, liability may be an issue. Shows can be stressful for many cats because of all the noise, activity, and physical touching. To reduce the risk of injuries to cats or humans, it's best to ask first and to respect the exhibitor's answer.

Give cats the right-of-way. Exhibitors are listening for their cats' numbers and need to get to judging rings on time. If you see someone carrying a cat and moving quickly down the aisle, step aside to let them both through.

Ask the exhibitors for permission before taking pictures of their cats. Most would be honored by such a request, but they may have important reasons for not allowing their cats' pictures to be taken. Respect their wishes.

Feel free to ask questions of judges, but only when they are not busy handling or evaluating cats. Although most judges love to answer questions and educate the public about pedigreed cats and the cat fancy in general, their first priority at the show is evaluating the competing cats. They also have a schedule to keep. Be respectful.

Cat shows are a fun and exciting opportunity to see some of the most beautiful cats around, and they provide a perfect opportunity to learn a great deal about your favorite breeds. Showing cats is a great hobby for you and your cat to enjoy together.

Feline Agility

A fairly new attraction that is gaining popularity at cat shows across the nation is feline agility competitions. Similar to the

Even a champion needs a little backstage play once in a while!

canine version where dogs climb ladders, jump through hoops, and wind around weave poles, cats can now show off their grace, athleticism, and talents as well.

In cat agility, exhibitors tempt their frisky felines through tunnels, over hurdles, around weave poles, and over ramps. Entrants are scored based on the best of several runs, including practice tries. The ultimate goal is for the cat to complete all the obstacles. Speed is used for tiebreakers.

This new cat competition is rapidly becoming a spectator favorite. Don't forget to check it out when you visit cat shows.

You are likely to find many exotic and beautiful breeds, such as this adorable Scottish fold, at cat shows.

Whether you choose a show-quality pedigreed cat or adopt a mixed breed, you will find a fun and loving companion in a kitten.

Appendix

Cat Registries

AMERICAN ASSOCIATION OF CAT ENTHUSIASTS (AACE)
PO Box 213
Pine Brook, NJ 07058
973-335-6717
http://www.aaceinc.org

AMERICAN CAT FANCIERS ASSOCIATION (ACFA)
PO Box 1949
Nixa, MO 65714-1949
417-725-1530
http://www.acfacats.com

CANADIAN CAT ASSOCIATION (CCA)
289 Rutherford Road, South, Unit 18
Brampton, Ontario, Canada L6W 3R9
905-459-1481
http://www.cca-afc.com

CAT FANCIERS' ASSOCIATION (CFA)
PO Box 1005
Manasquan, NJ 08736-0805
732-528-9797
http://www.cfa.org

CAT FANCIERS' FEDERATION (CFF)
PO Box 661
Gratis, OH 45330
937-787-9009
http://www.cffinc.org

THE INTERNATIONAL CAT ASSOCIATION (TICA)
PO Box 2684
Harlingen, TX 78551
956-428-8046
http://www.tica.org

NATIONAL CAT FANCIERS' ASSOCIATION (NCFA)
10215 W. Mount Morris Road
Flushing, MI 48433
810-659-9517

TRADITIONAL CAT ASSOCIATION (TCA)
PO Box 178
Heisson, WA 98622-0178
http://www.traditionalcats.com

UNITED FELINE ORGANIZATION (UFO)
218 N.W. 180th Street
Newberry, FL 32669
352-472-4701

Helpful Resources

ACADEMY OF VETERINARY HOMEOPATHY
PO Box 9280
Wilmington, DE 19809
866-652-1590
http://www.theavh.org

ALLEY CAT ALLIES (ACA)
1801 Belmont Road N.W., Suite 201
Washington, DC 20009
202-667-3630
http://www.alleycat.org

AMERICAN ANIMAL HOSPITAL ASSOCIATION (AAHA)
12575 W. Bayaud Ave.
Lakewood, CO 80228
303-986-2800
http://www.healthypet.com or http://www.aahanet.org

AMERICAN ASSOCIATION OF FEED CONTROL OFFICIALS
(AAFCO)
http://www.aafco.org

AMERICAN ASSOCIATION OF FELINE PRACTITIONERS
(AAFP)
203 Towne Centre Drive
Hillsborough, NJ 08844-4693
800-204-3414
http://www.aafponline.org

AMERICAN HOLISTIC VETERINARY MEDICAL
ASSOCIATION (AHVMA)
2218 Old Emmorton Road
Bel Air, MD 21015
410-569-0795
http://www.ahvma.org

AMERICAN HUMANE ASSOCIATION (AHA)
Animal Services
6 Inverness Drive E
Englewood, CO 80112
866-242-1877
http://www.americanhumane.org

AMERICAN SOCIETY FOR THE PREVENTION OF
CRUELTY TO ANIMALS (ASPCA)
424 E. 92nd Street
New York, NY 10128-6804
212-876-7700
http://www.aspca.org

AMERICAN VETERINARY MEDICAL ASSOCIATION
(AVMA)
1931 N. Meacham Road, Suite 100
Schaumburg, IL 60173-4360
800-248-2862
http://www.avma.org

BEST FRIENDS ANIMAL SOCIETY
5001 Angel Canyon Road
Kanab, UT 84741
435-644-2001
http://www.bestfriends.org

CAT FANCY MAGAZINE
PO Box 6050
Mission Viejo, CA 92690-6050
949-855-8822
http://www.catfancy.com

THE DELTA SOCIETY
580 Naches Ave. S.W., Suite 101
Renton, WA 98055-2297
425-226-7357
http://www.deltasociety.org

DORIS DAY ANIMAL LEAGUE
227 Massachusetts Ave. N.E., Suite 100
Washington, DC 20002
202-546-1761
http://www.ddal.org

FUND FOR ANIMALS INC.
200 W. 57th Street
New York, NY 10019
212-246-2096
http://www.fund.org

HUMANE SOCIETY OF THE UNITED STATES (HSUS)
2100 L Street N.W.
Washington, DC 20037
202-452-1100
http://www.hsus.org

INTERNATIONAL VETERINARY ACUPUNCTURE
SOCIETY
P.O. Box 271395
Fort Collins, CO 80527-1395
970-266-0666
http://www.ivas.org/main.cf

MORRIS ANIMAL FOUNDATION
Public Relations Dept.
45 Inverness Drive E.
Englewood, CO 80112-5480
800-243-2345
http://www.morrisanimalfoundation.org

NATIONAL ASSOCIATION OF PROFESSIONAL PET SITTERS
17000 Commerce Pkwy., Suite C
Mt. Laurel, NJ 08054
800-296-PETS
http://www.petsitters.org

THE NIKKI HOSPICE FOUNDATION FOR PETS
400 New Bedford Drive
Vallejo, CA 94591
707-557-8595
http://www.pethospice.org

PET SITTERS INTERNATIONAL
201 E. King St.
King, NC 27021
336-983-9222
http://www.petsit.com

SPAY/USA
2261 Broadbridge Ave.
Stratford, CT 06614
800-248-7729
http://www.spayusa.org

THE WINN FELINE FOUNDATION
1805 Atlantic Ave.
Manasquan, NJ 07836-0805
732-528-9797
http://www.winnfelinehealth.org

Hotlines

ASPCA
212-876-7700

ASPCA ANIMAL POISON CONTROL CENTER
(formerly National Animal Poison Control Center)
888-426-4435

Glossary

alter: an altered (spayed or neutered) cat

breeder: someone who owns pedigreed cats and breeds them to continue the line and integrity of the breed

breed standard: the ideal physical characteristics for a particular breed, as agreed upon by a group of breeders and standardized by a registration association

cat fancy: the individual people, clubs, and registration associations involved with breeding and showing cats

cattery: a group of cats in a breeding or boarding program; sometimes this term also refers to the physical structure in which a group of cats live

championship: a class at North American shows that is open to unaltered, pedigreed adult cats who meet the standard for their breed

coat: a cat's fur

disqualification: a physical quality that makes a cat ineligible for show, according to the cat's breed standard

household pet (HHP): a North American class open to all cats who are not eligible to compete in any other class kitten: a young, immature cat, or the class at North American shows that is open to pedigreed kittens between four and eight months old

longhair: a cat with relatively long hair

neuter: to castrate a male cat

open: a cat who has not achieved Champion status

pedigree: a document that records a cat's ancestors

pedigreed cat: a cat with a pedigree

points: units that a cat accumulates during a show; once a certain number of points are gained, the cat receives a specific title or award (each association has its own way of determining and awarding points)

purebred: a cat whose ancestors are all in the same breed, according to the breed standard

registered cat: a cat whose ancestry can be verified through documentation and is recorded with a cat registering association

ring: an area at a cat show where a judge examines cats and awards prizes; most shows have several concurrently active rings

shorthair: a cat with relatively short hair

show: a place where cats are displayed and evaluated by all-breed or specialty judges and awarded prizes

spay: the surgical removal of a female cat's reproductive organs

standard: an agreed-upon regulation governing aspects of a cat breed's physical appearance

Index

The Complete Care Made Easy™ Series

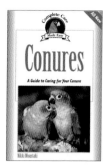

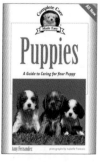